From Nun to Priest

Hope for Those Bound By Tradition

From **Nun** *to* **Priest**

Hope for Those Bound By Tradition

Joanne A. Howe
Author of *"A Change of Habit"*

CHRISTIAN
COMMUNICATIONS

Published by Christian Communications
PO Box 150, Nashville, TN 37202

ISBN 0-89225-451-3

Dedication

This book is affectionately dedicated to each and every former Catholic, who because of the courage of their convictions and the love of God, walked in faith and accepted Jesus alone as their Lord and Savior. I look forward to greeting you before the throne of God.

Praise the God of our salvation, for His great love endures forever!

Acknowledgments

⋄⋄⋄

The author wishes to acknowledge the invaluable assistance and support of the following people:

The Family of God throughout the United States and abroad for believing in the importance of this message;

Dr. Truman Scott for his knowledge, insight and vision;

Lydia Holby who graciously donated hours of her time to transfer this manuscript to disk;

Odell Lee, elder at the Fairfax church of Christ, for his valuable editorial contributions;

Dr. Matthias Samu, a former Catholic priest, for his generous comments;

and my family for their love and suggestions.

My greatest appreciation goes to my Heavenly Father, who made all things work together so His name alone is glorified and His teachings exalted.

Foreword

There must have been an angel sitting on her shoulder as Joanne Howe wrote this book. For how else could she weave for us so skillfully the forces at work in the three major stages of her personal saga? First, her total devotion as a child and young adult to a religious order, to its rituals, disciplines, and traditions. Second, at age 32 her acceptance that she was disillusioned, uncertain, and spiritually barren. And third, her journey to discover as she found the voice of God speaking to her through the scriptures of the Bible.

That journey continues. In *From Nun to Priest*, Joanne has knit together innumerable strands of memory, feelings, research, personal correspondence, and Bible passages to let us follow her. We are the richer for it.

Joanne Howe has written this book to be read by all those who seek what she has always sought — the path of righteousness. That makes it a rare book.

But then, she is a rare person.

Marion Barnette
Mobile, Alabama

Table of Contents

Introduction

∽◯∾

Shortly after my conversion to the "Good News of the Gospel," I traveled home to Pittsburgh, Pennsylvania, to visit with my parents and share with them my acceptance of New Testament Christianity. I can still see my father's pained face and hear his concerned response as he said, "Joanne, I was born a Catholic, and I will die a Catholic. No matter what choice you have made, I will always remain faithful to my Catholic religion." True to his word, my father went to eternity maintaining his profession in Roman Catholicism.

Remembering my father's position and that of many other faithful Catholics I have met in my pilgrim journey toward eternity, I have sought numerous ways to share with them the message God wrote for them in His Word — the Bible. Many with whom I have spoken do not believe in the Bible nor in the existence of absolute truth. They believe that all truth is relative and that what may be true for one is not true for another. Combine this attitude with the popular mindset that each of us must take care of "Number One" first and truth then becomes simply that which makes you happy today.

I am a believer in the Bible as God's Word. I accept God's teachings as absolute. I understand that truth is knowable and that the Scriptures are truth. What I believe and how I live are important. Consequently, I must submit my feelings, experiences, and circumstances to God's truth. In this light, the writing of this book took on great importance for me. As a former nun of 19 years with the Sisters of St. Joseph from Baden, Pennsylvania, I was dedicated to teaching Catholics the doctrines and traditions of their faith. Today, as one of God's royal priests (1 Peter 2:9), I am just as committed to teaching Catholics the biblical errors in their religion and present to them God's plan for them in this life, as well as His plan for their eternity. I have long felt a need for a book of this nature for Catholics to read.

The purpose of this book, therefore, is not to stir up hatred, discord, or strife. There has been enough Catholic-bashing throughout the centuries. Rather, it is to call attention to biblical errors I discovered in the teachings and traditions of my former faith, Roman Catholicism. I want this book to accomplish two very modest tasks: (1) to guide the Catholic who wants to be introduced to biblical truths and (2) to help individuals who are inquiring in their own way, with regard to their choice for eternity. Every effort has been made to use terminology that can be easily understood by every reader.

It is my desire that this book will bring hope to wounded and spiritually starved Catholics. I am well aware that many of my former people have been oppressed by those in the Catholic hierarchy. Although a form of renewal is going on in Roman Catholicism today, there are many indications that these changes are merely cosmetic. Therefore, this book is primarily directed to those individuals who find themselves uninformed and bewildered by these changes. The masses of Roman Catholics are honest and sincere. I believe that if they knew the facts they would be among the first to rebel against the teachings and traditions of their faith. Of course, it is the reader's prerogative to judge whether or not the conclusions I have drawn in the following pages are justified. However, this book will have served its purpose if it stimulates honest thought and if the reader obeys what God has to say from the pages of His Holy Word. In conclusion, what Paul says in his letter to the churches in Galatia is relative to the message of this book. He writes:

> I marvel that you are turning away so soon from Him who called you in the grace of Christ, to a different gospel, which is not another; but there are some who trouble you and want to pervert the gospel of Christ. But even if we, or an angel from heaven, preach any other gospel to you than what we have preached to you, let him be accursed (Galatians 1:6-8).

A Change of Habit —
Looking Back

October 4, 1972, will always stand out in my memory as the day of my new birth. The excitement and anxiety I felt that morning swelled to disproportionate heights as I stepped from the pew in which I was sitting and walked down the aisle to give myself to God in the waters of baptism. Before this special day, I had lived through my youth and young adulthood in search of truth. On this day I now found myself at this crossroads: Should I remain faithful to the teachings and traditions of Roman Catholicism or should I accept the teachings of the Bible as my sole directive in life. I knew in my heart that if I did not give myself totally to Jesus in the waters of baptism I would turn my back on Him completely and return to the religion of my parents — Roman Catholicism.

The distance from the pew to the front of the auditorium resonated from tension within me. My mind reverted to another special day some 15 years before this significant occasion. On August 19, 1959, I stepped forward to take my final vows before God as a nun with the Sisters of St. Joseph from Baden, Pennsylvania. Before the entire community, I promised "to honor and keep the vows of poverty, chastity and obedience according to the rules of the congregation and under the guidance of the superiors in charge."

Fifteen years had now passed since I had taken those vows. During this interim, I had gone through a crisis of spirituality and of self-identity. I had grown up in a tightly knit Catholic community of family, friends, and relatives accepting and believing the doctrines set forth in the Baltimore Catechism. The one value I carried with me throughout my formative years was the belief that having been born into a Roman Catholic family was the greatest of all earthly blessings.

As a young child, I was taught and I believed that becoming a nun was a special privilege — an earned-in-heaven reward, a mark of distinction. Throughout my childhood, I sought ways of developing a deeper relationship with God. In 1949, I entered a preparatory school for girls desirous of dedicating their lives to God as religious nuns.

Seeking to gain favor in the eyes of my family, the church, and God, I then chose to enter the religious order of the Sisters of St. Joseph in 1953, and I remained in this community until 1968. During my last two years in this religious order, I sought professional help from a Christian psychologist. We both concluded that I had not given God His rightful place in my heart (although I had no idea how this could be accomplished) and that I should leave the convent.

Returning to society after three years in a preparatory school and 16 years in the religious order left me unprepared for the challenges that lay ahead. First, came the pressure of conformity to a society and its customs I knew little or nothing about. I had been limited in the use of money. Consequently, I was ignorant about keeping a budget. My selection of clothing and hair style centered primarily on the suggestions of elderly women with whom I worked or met at church. Next, came the pressure to conform to the new values that were crashing in all around me. Since my opportunities to enjoy a relationship with the opposite sex had been non-existent, I felt awkward in communicating with the men I would date occasionally. The new morality that exploded in the '60s had revolutionized sexual relationships. Consequently, the sexual demands placed upon me created an anxiety much worse that I had known or experienced in convent life. Superseding any other concern that might have troubled me about the society I had chosen to return to was my quest for self-identity. I struggled to discover who I was as a woman, a member of society, a child of God, and my own person. I walked out of the door of convent life believing I would find acceptance, affection, approval, and a true course to follow. Instead I found difficult choices and many disappointments.

Raised in the era of pre-Vatical Roman Catholicism, I believed the teachings and traditions of the church were omniscient. Everything I learned and believed created in my psyche an absolute certainty of faith. Knowing that more than 17 percent of the world's population and 25 percent of the U.S. population were Catholic, I was proud of the universality of my religious heritage. I was convinced that Catholicism was the only road to God and that the only faithful people singing praise to God in Heaven would be Roman Catholics.

Discovery is no quick fix. It is a process that occurs over a period of time, sometimes ranging from months to years. Because of the incredible marks of tradition and doctrine that were imblazened on my heart and mind in my early formative years as a Catholic I sought for a deeper meaning of life and a closer walk with God. I was unaware that this close relationship could only occur by breaking the bondage to sin that existed in my heart and by unraveling the hurts and deceptive teachings and traditions I had woven around it. I was to discover this process by admitting the enslavement I had succumbed to through blindly adhering to traditions and unbiblical teachings throughout my life as a Roman Catholic and by admitting my deepest needs — the need to belong and the need to be needed by significant others in my life.

My initial personal encounter with the Word of God and its power to provide freedom from my bondage came at a professional counseling session with a preacher of the Gospel. I had been introduced to this individual through a fellow teacher. She arranged for me to meet with Paul Coffman.

After listening to my painful crises, both emotional and spiritual, he said, "Joanne, the answers to all of your problems and anxieties are given in God's Word." Picking up the Bible from his desk, he added, "The Bible will tell you who you are, where you are going, and how you will get there!" This statement gave life to a spiritual genesis in my relationship with God and others. These relationships were to evolve into the ultimate choices I would make as to my lifestyle here on this earth and my eternal destiny.

Each week I learned more about how to identify with the ingredients of a healthy self-concept. I realized the depth of my pain and the self-destructive course I had programmed for myself because of unrepented sin and ingrained sinful habits. My self-esteem, self-worth, self-image, and self-acceptance projected inadequacy and worthlessness. I was desperate to find inner fulfillment and peace of mind. Nothing had occupied more of my time than the attempt to appease the restlessness and discontent that existed in my soul. Always believing I was a seeker of truth, I made the decision to investigate the claims that were presented to me about God and my relationship with Him in His Word.

My previous exposure to biblical teachings was of a historical nature and scholarly in their presentation. Part of the curriculum in the Catholic educational program was Bible history. I learned about the lives of many biblical characters through the stories that were presented in a series of lessons in these classes. "The Bible," I was told, "was a book to be read and interpreted by those in ecclesiastical authority." Any individual interpretation was strongly discouraged by those in the Roman Catholic hierarchy.

Although I knew that the Bible was the world's best-selling book, I couldn't explain the purpose of its message, nor did I understand why it was written. The contents of both the Old and New Testaments were mystifying in their teachings and overwhelming in the information they conveyed. Because I had never been taught how to read the Bible or how to understand its message, I felt woefully ignorant of God's purpose for having it written. When I was told that it would tell me who I was, where I was going, and how I would arrive at my destination, I was confused and concerned that I had never received any instruction like this as a Roman Catholic. I had always depended on the Catholic Church's directives to lead me in ways in which I could serve and glorify God and eventually earn my salvation.

After each counseling session, I would devote time to studying God's Word personally. Opening the Bible to Psalms in the Old Testament, I read the following:

> The law of the LORD is perfect, converting the soul;
> The testimony of the LORD is sure, making wise the
> simple; The statutes of the LORD are right, rejoicing
> the heart; The commandment of the LORD is pure,
> enlightening the eyes; The fear of the LORD is clean,
> enduring forever; The judgments of the LORD are
> true and righteous altogether (Psalm. 19:7-9).

I saw from this passage that it was important to discover God's truths and His laws in my search for a closer relationship with Him. My life needed meaning, and I desperately needed His words of comfort to ease my pain and guilt. As I continued my study of God's Word and His relationship to me, I discovered this assurance in Jeremiah 29:13: "And you will seek Me and find Me, when you search for Me with all your heart."

Throughout my years of training in the theology of Roman Catholicism, I had known God as the great, glorious, and independent source of all life, wisdom, power, and knowledge. Now, I was reading breathtaking concepts of God and of His perfect knowledge of all things past, present, and future. I knew that God is not limited by or to time and space. I had learned many years before that God is unchanging and perfectly righteous in all His doings. This was now confirmed as I read David's description of God in 1 Chronicles 29:10-13:

> Blessed are You, LORD God of Israel, our Father, forever and ever. Yours, O LORD, is the greatness, The power and the glory, The victory and the majesty; For all that is in heaven and in earth is Yours; Yours is the kingdom, O LORD, And You are exalted as head over all. Both riches and honor come from You, And You reign over all. In Your hand is power and might; In Your hand it is to make great And to give strength to all. Now therefore, our God, We thank You And praise Your glorious name.

In Job 22:21 I read: "Now acquaint yourself with Him, and be at peace." Throughout my years as a nun, I had always considered it a high calling and a privilege to serve God and glorify Him in the vocation I had chosen. During the counseling process I was told that God wanted me to come to know Him personally and intimately. God wanted me to know how much He loves me and how much He cares for me. He wanted me to know that He is good, full of compassion, lovingkindness, and mercy. He is concerned for my personal well-being. God wanted me to know that he is faithful and unchanging. God also wanted me to know that He tenderly yearns and cares for me as a mother cares for her child and that when I am tempted, fearful, anxious, or discouraged I must trust Him to comfort me. Psalm 9:10 says this so eloquently: "And those who know Your name will put their trust in You; For You, LORD, have not forsaken those who seek You."

In Jeremiah 9:24, I read God's thoughts on knowing Him:

"But let him who glories glory in this, That he understands and knows Me, That I am the LORD, exercising lovingkindness, judgment, and righteousness in the earth. For in these I delight," says the LORD.

Getting to know God requires a decisive and total commitment. I wanted desperately to integrate my life into His. Thus it became the chief purpose and aim of my life to know God. Since I had always been taught I was on this earth because of God's great love for me, I knew in the depths of my heart that true joy, peace, and fullness of life could only be experienced when I learned to know God more intimately and trusted Him more completely.

In Genesis 1:26-27, God told me that I was the crowning point of His creation with special power and authority. I read about the unique privilege of being created in the image of God with a mind to think, to understand, to will, to love, and to choose:

Then God said, "Let Us make man in Our image, according to Our likeness; let them have dominion over the fish of the sea, over the birds of the air, and over the cattle, over all the earth and over every creeping thing that creeps on the earth." So God created man in His own image; in the image of God He created him; male and female He created them.

In Isaiah, God explains why I have been created, why I have been redeemed, and why He has uniquely designed me. He says:

"Everyone who is called by My name, Whom I have created for My glory; I have formed him, yes, I have made him ... You are My witnesses," says the LORD, "And My servant whom I have chosen, That you may know and believe Me, And understand that I am He ... I, even I, am the LORD, And besides Me there is no savior ... This people I have formed for Myself; They shall declare My praise" (Isaiah 43:7, 10-11, 21).

To know and believe I was loved engendered the deepest kind of soul-satisfaction. To know and believe that God loved me unconditionally brought tears of gratitude and humility. In Jeremiah 31:3, I read these comforting words: "Yes, I have loved you with an everlasting love; Therefore with lovingkindness I have drawn you."

Seeing myself from God's perspective was to realize that underneath all my sin, temptations, and confusion, the image of God existed in me, and no matter how often I fell short God's love would triumph. I rejoiced to know that God's attitude toward me is one of constant encouragement and support. Throughout Scripture I read where the human race is significant, yet sinful. Until I recognized the truth of my significance and understood God through His holiness, justice, love, and goodness, I would not be able to deal meaningfully with the problems of guilt and the sinful choices I had made in my life.

There were many references in the Bible where God told me that He not only made me as His special creation to live in fellowship with Him but also gave me freedom of choice. In Genesis 2:17, I read where my first ancestors abused this freedom and disobeyed God when He gave them His first negative commandment:

> "[B]ut of the tree of the knowledge of good and evil you shall not eat, for in the day that you eat of it you shall surely die."

When Adam and Eve disobeyed God, their relationship and that of their descendants was broken with God. The broken commandment meant broken communion with God. Because of their disobedience God told them that they and their descendants would become victims of disease, decay, and deterioration. Adam and Eve had been two living souls in touch and in tune with God — innocent and immortal. After their disobedience they were dead souls in dying bodies. Their story ends with three inevitable words: "[A]nd he [Adam] died" (Genesis 5:5).

As a small child, I recall learning from my Baltimore Catechism that I was a descendant of Adam. He and Eve were cut off from God, separated by sin. Consequently my life was in the same condition. In reading God's Word, it was repeatedly made clear to me that I too had chosen to become a sinner.

My greatest desire was to get my heart right with God. I knew and understood that before a holy and righteous God I was responsible for every sin I had ever committed. In Romans 3:23 I read: "[F]or all have sinned and fall short of the glory of God."

Therefore, I could not have confidence in my flesh and I was helpless to save myself. Adam's blood runs through my veins! Through Adam's sin, I inherited a predisposition to sin. Consequently, my soul was dead because of my own sins. God's Word confirms this in Romans 5:12:

> Therefore, just as through one man sin entered the world, and death through sin, and thus death spread to all men, because all sinned.

In that passage, God's Word also tells me that as long as I am in the flesh it is impossible to avoid all sin. John said in 1 John 1:8, "If we say that we have no sin, we deceive ourselves, and the truth is not in us."

Because of my nature and the personal choice I made to sin (a determination to go my own way) I became alienated from God. As a result, my fellowship with Him was cut off. His design for me to reflect His image and bring glory to His name was short-circuited. Deeply sorrowful and wanting to restore my relationship with my Creator, I asked a crucial question: "How can I become reconciled with a God who loves me so deeply and has done so much for me?"

God arranged a way for my debt to Him to be paid so I could stand justified (just as if I had not sinned) before His holy and pure Deity. In Romans 6:1-4, I read these consoling words:

What shall we say then? Shall we continue in sin that grace may abound? Certainly not! How shall we who died to sin live any longer in it? Or do you not know that as many of us as were baptized into Christ Jesus were baptized into His death? Therefore we were buried with Him through baptism into death, that just as Christ was raised from the dead by the glory of the Father, even so we also should walk in newness of life.

God's Word, from beginning to end, showed me that to be right with Him I needed to follow His simple plan. I was shown in His Word I was a sinner, I was spiritually dead, and I was separated from God. Jesus died for me that I might have my spiritual life with God restored. After Jesus rose from the dead but before His ascension, Jesus charged His apostles:

"Go therefore and make disciples of all the nations, baptizing them in the name of the Father and of the Son and of the Holy Spirit" (Matthew 28:19).

Although I was baptized as an infant, I was compelled to decide for myself, as an adult before God, whether this infant baptism satisfied my obedience to this divine command.

I was now at the central crossroads of my life! By a simple act of obedience, I could walk in newness of life with my Creator. I wanted to be relieved of my load of guilt. I didn't want to worry about facing the consequences of my sins in eternity. I had no choice now but to choose God's way and become immersed in the waters of baptism for the remission of my sins. I reflected on the 36 years I had spent on the other side of the Cross — religious, but not right with God. I had been deluded into believing that performing religious acts would earn me the right and privilege of going to heaven. I truly thought if I did the best I could, treated everyone fairly, and kept the Ten Commandments I would be assured of eternity.

Coming to grips with one's ideologies and religious convictions is challenging and traumatic. Change is never easy. It demands risk and courage. It touches the gray matter of the unknown. It rattles securities one has become accustomed to over a period of time, for the old ways are so secure and comfortable. It is painful to change and discard habits that have become so engrained in one's beliefs and behaviors. My deep faith in and commitment to God started the salvation process in my life. The power of the Word of God took hold of my mind and began to change my thinking and purpose for life.

As I walked down the aisle that memorable day in October 1972 to give my life to God and accept His offer of forgiveness, I could see His outreached arms of love and forgiveness and hear Him saying:

"Behold, I stand at the door and knock. If anyone hears My voice and opens the door, I will come in to him and dine with him, and he with Me" (Revelation 3:20).

I will never forget the joy of that occasion! Of all the public professions of my love and commitment to God, this event was explosive — in my heart and in the portals of heaven. I knew this was only the beginning of my journey. Just as the waters of baptism had immersed my physical body, my soul was immersed in the cleansing blood of Jesus. I now wanted my inner-spirit to become saturated with each truth in God's Word and know His will for every aspect of my life.

Departure From Roman Catholicism and Acceptance of New Testament Christianity

Stepping away from the teaching of my parents and accepting the authority of the Bible was a decision that would change my whole relationship with God and my earthly family as well.

Growing up with a Catholic heritage was a matter of having been born of Catholic parents, baptized as an infant into the faith, obeying implicitly all the teachings of canon law, and honoring all the traditions required by those in authority. These teachings were to be the core of my moral and ethical value system throughout my youth and young adulthood. I was taught the intellectual and emotional acceptance of a set of dogmas that I was assured would help me to develop a deeper prayer life and a Catholic attitude. I was never to question the doctrines of my faith. It was not until the Second Vatican Council convened in 1962 that the searching process was condoned and a sense of individualism was encouraged.

Every Catholic child who attended a parochial school was expected to know the main purpose and the importance of the Mass. I learned early in my Catholic education that the

Mass is the center of Catholic worship and the heart of a Catholic's life. The Mass is considered the same sacrifice as the sacrifice of the cross. I was told that the only difference between the two was that the cross was a bloody sacrifice and the Mass was an unbloody sacrifice. My mind was trained to become emotionally involved with Jesus' death, especially during the sacrifice of the Mass. I was taught that shortly before our Savior's death, He established the sacrifice of the Mass at His last supper. In this sacrifice, there was to be no new death of our Savior, but His death was to be represented vividly by the twofold consecration of the bread into His body and the wine into His blood. This act, I learned, was called the process of "transubstantiation" or the "real presence."

The idea that the sacrifice of the Mass was the greatest possible act of worship to God always created a deep reverence within me during this ceremony. Attending Mass was one of the most important duties of my Catholic religion. I remember being told that the more fervently I participated in the offering of the Mass, the more blessings I would receive from my crucified Savior. Consequently, I attended Mass as often as possible in order to receive many extra blessings.

One of the most important doctrines of the Catholic faith is the "Sacrament of the Eucharist." According to the Baltimore Catechism, this sacrament is the means provided by God and by the Church to perform one's duties as a faithful Catholic and to save one's soul. I was taught that a sacrament gives grace, through power which it possesses, to sanctify the soul as an instrument of God. The word "Eucharist" means "to give thanks." God has an immense love for every soul He creates. He gave proof of this by shedding His Son's precious blood for the salvation of mankind. The Catholic doctrine of the Eucharist teaches that after Jesus' death, resurrection, and ascension into heaven, He could no longer associate intimately with those He loved. Therefore, Jesus devised a means whereby He could still remain on earth, not merely in one place but in every church where His faithful attended.

This is supposedly accomplished through the process of transubstantiation, which literally means "change of substance." I was taught that through the power of the priest, invested upon him at his ordination to the priesthood, the divinity of Christ appears in the physical elements of bread and wine. This occurs during the Mass when the priest repeats the words Jesus spoke at His last supper: "This is my body; this is my blood." I recall that it was strongly enforced that I was not to question "how" Jesus could be present under the appearances of bread and wine, but it was my duty to have faith that this actually occurred.

In tender-hearted, wide-eyed wonder, I gloried in every opportunity provided for me to receive the actual body and blood of Jesus in the form of a small white wafer. Before partaking of the Eucharist, I was to fast from food and water from midnight on Saturday until the next morning. Upon receiving Jesus in my heart, I was forbidden to let the wafer touch the roof of my mouth. In other words, I was not to chew the body and blood of Christ but let him dissolve slowly in my mouth. When this wafer was fully consumed, the presence of Jesus would be in my heart to help me and console me in the difficulties and temptations of my journey through life.

Before becoming scripturally baptized, I took the time to look through a Bible concordance — an alphabetical index of where principle words appear in the Bible — to justify the teachings and traditions I had believed and had taught as a nun. I had hoped to find scripture references that would authenticate the main doctrine of all Catholic worship — the Mass. I hoped to verify the teaching that the "Sacrifice of the Mass" is the greatest possible act of divine worship and the only form of sacrifice acceptable to God after His Son's death.

I looked for every occurrence in the New Testament of the words "Mass" and "Eucharistic Sacrifice," and I made an astounding discovery! Not one scripture referred to the word "Mass" or "Eucharistic Sacrifice." This left me feeling misled and disillusioned as a committed Roman Catholic.

In the Acts of the Apostles and in the Epistles, I read of prayer, praise, and the preaching of the Gospel as the works designated by Christ to carry out His ministry. Not one of these included offering the "Sacrifice of the Mass." In Hebrews I read where the Scriptures declared that there was only one sacrifice:

> [He] who does not need daily, as those high priests, to offer up sacrifices, first for His own sins and then for the people's, for this He did once for all when He offered up Himself (Hebrews 7:27).

> And as it is appointed for men to die once, but after this the judgment, so Christ was offered once to bear the sins of many (Hebrews 9:27-28).

I read that there is no need to repeat any other sacrifice for our sins:

> By that will we have been sanctified through the offering of the body of Jesus Christ once for all ... For by one offering He has perfected forever those who are being sanctified (Hebrews 10:10, 14).

These scriptures contained proof beyond doubt that Jesus offered one sacrifice that was adequate in obtaining for me the full pardon of my sin. Once my sins had been forgiven there was no longer any need for further sacrifice. These scriptures showed me the superiority of both the priesthood and the sacrifice of Jesus.

In 1 Peter 2:5, Peter stressed the only type of sacrifice that was necessary to offer to God:

> [Y]ou also, as living stones, are being built up a spiritual house, a holy priesthood, to offer up spiritual sacrifices acceptable to God through Jesus Christ.

In Hebrews 13:15-16 I read the following passage that once again identified the kind of sacrifice God would honor:

> Therefore by Him let us continually offer the sacrifice of praise to God, that is, the fruit of our lips, giving thanks to His name. But do not forget to do good and to share, for with such sacrifices God is well pleased.

Hoping to alleviate further frustration and confusion, I then sought to find the words "Eucharist" or "Holy Communion" in the New Testament. In an apologetics class, I had learned that the sixth chapter of John contained the magnificent bread of life discourse which gave me background on how to understand this Eucharistic meal of Christ. Out of great reverence for this sacrament, I knew I would discover the Eucharist had been ordained by God in His holy Word. I had been taught to have deep regard for the Bible, and I would listen in awe whenever it was read from the pulpit during the Mass. I investigated the words of Jesus in John 6:47-58:

> "Most assuredly, I say to you, he who believes in Me has everlasting life. I am the bread of life. Your fathers ate the manna in the wilderness, and are dead. This is the bread which comes down from heaven, that one may eat of it and not die. I am the living bread which came down from heaven. If anyone eats of this bread, he will live forever; and the bread that I shall give is My flesh, which I shall give for the life of the world." The Jews therefore quarreled among themselves, saying, "How can this Man give us His flesh to eat?" Then Jesus said to them, "Most assuredly, I say to you, unless you eat the flesh of the Son of Man and drink His blood, you have no life in you. Whoever eats My flesh and drinks My blood has eternal life, and I will raise him up at the last day. For My flesh is food indeed, and My blood is drink indeed. He who eats My flesh and drinks My blood abides in Me, and I in

him. As the living Father sent Me, and I live because
of the Father, so he who feeds on Me will live because
of Me. This is the bread which came down from
heaven — not as your fathers ate the manna, and are
dead. He who eats this bread will live forever."

In reading and re-reading this passage, I began to see the
significance of what Jesus said. In verse 47, Jesus has shown
that life eternal is obtainable only through Him. This is
also taught in John 3:15: "that whoever believes in Him
should not perish but have eternal life."

Human life is sustained by eating physical bread, as the
Jews were sustained when they ate the manna in the desert.
However, Jesus referred to the "bread which comes down
out of heaven" as sustaining the spiritual life of the inner
man. Jesus was saying He is that bread and there is no other.
Anyone who chooses to embrace Him as the "bread of life"
will live forever. Jesus did not say that we were to dine on His
body but rather reaffirmed the underlying principle of this
"living bread." It is imperishable and completely satisfying.

I imagine the Jews could not understand the symbolic
nature of Jesus' teachings because of their prejudice and
unbelief. Had they opened their minds and hearts, as I did,
they would have come to the same conclusion as I did. The
steps by which Jesus taught this marvelous truth are very
clear and vivid. Jesus is the "life of men," being both the
source and the preserver of it. Jesus is the "bread of life,"
always satisfying the hunger of men. Jesus is the "water of
life," and those who drink it will never thirst again. In John
4:14 Jesus says:

> "[B]ut whoever drinks of the water that I shall give
> him will never thirst. But the water that I shall give
> him will become in him a fountain of water spring-
> ing up into everlasting life."

Every scripture that speaks of eating Jesus' flesh and
drinking His blood (Matthew 26:26-29 and 1 Corinthians

11:23-29) refers to abiding in Jesus, accepting His teachings, and obeying His will. When this occurs, mankind can have spiritual fellowship with Him and will never hunger, thirst, or die a spiritual death in eternity.

For centuries, the Roman Catholic Church has presented many of its teachings that are unexplainable as "Theological Mysteries." In my theology classes I learned that a "Theological Mystery" is a hidden or secret thing of a sacred character. I was told that those teachings in Roman Catholicism that are mysteries can only be known by revelation, and even when a mystery is revealed and believed, it remains obscure and veiled in this life. Thus, in the Mass, immediately following the consecration of the bread, the priest says to the laity, "Let us proclaim the mystery of faith." Catholics are taught that faith itself is a gift of God and one must be properly disposed to receive it with an open mind.

The deep faith I had as a Catholic and a Christian today, I owe to my early upbringing in Roman Catholicism. As an adult, my faith and loyalty to God have never wavered, but my pursuit for timeless truth was discovered in God's Word.

Being reared as a strong and committed Catholic, I believed without question those doctrines in the Baltimore Catechism that claimed to be biblical in their contents and origins. My personal faith was not established on scientific philosophies or biblical knowledge but on what I believed in my heart to be truth. Nothing in my life was more important to me than being right with God. While doing research on doctrines taught to me in Roman Catholicism that were said to be of biblical origin, I came upon this passage in Romans:

> So, as much as is in me, I am ready to preach the gospel to you who are in Rome also. For I am not ashamed of the gospel of Christ, for it is the power of God to salvation for everyone who believes, for the Jew first and also for the Greek. For in it the righteousness of God is

revealed from faith to faith; as it is written, "The just shall live by faith" (Romans 1:15-17).

I questioned, "How does God put me right with Himself?" Paul revealed this to me in the third chapter of Romans:

> But now the righteousness of God apart from the law is revealed, being witnessed by the Law and the Prophets, even the righteousness of God, through faith in Jesus Christ, to all and on all who believe. For there is no difference; for all have sinned and fall short of the glory of God, being justified freely by His grace through the redemption that is in Christ Jesus, whom God set forth as a propitiation by His blood, through faith, to demonstrate His righteousness, because in His forbearance God had passed over the sins that were previously committed, to demonstrate at the present time His righteousness, that He might be just and the justifier of the one who has faith in Jesus (Romans 3:21-26).

One particular part of this passage stood out more than any other. Our righteousness with God was not through the law of Moses! Throughout my life as a Roman Catholic I had attempted to follow God's Ten Commandments. These laws guided my behavior and duties toward God. I was taught as a very small child that besides believing and obeying the laws of the Catholic Church, I was to keep the Ten Commandments which God gave to Moses on Mt. Sinai. I remember being told that Jesus did away with all the Jewish ceremonial laws, but my obedience to the Ten Commandments was the surest way of winning the happiness of heaven. Upon reading the third chapter of Romans, I was now uncertain of my spiritual status before God. Once again, I began to cross-reference scriptures that related to the "law of Moses" and "sin" in the New Testament. I came upon a significant passage in Colossians where Paul speaks about Christ's work:

[H]aving wiped out the handwriting of requirements
that was against us, which was contrary to us. And
He has taken it out of the way, having nailed it to the
cross (Colossians 2:14).

I was now just beginning to understand that not one soul
was saved by keeping the law of Moses. Only one person
kept that law completely — Jesus. It is only through Jesus'
perfect sacrifice that all mankind, including those under
the law, can be saved. No man's sins could be forgiven by
the sacrifices under the law of Moses — forgiveness could
come only with the perfect sacrifice of Jesus, the Son of God.
It was hard for me to believe that the law of Moses had been
nailed to the cross. I now understood that to depend on the
law of Moses actually served as an obstacle to obtaining
forgiveness — for forgiveness was found only in Jesus.

I sincerely wanted to follow God's plan for salvation. I knew
I was a sinner. As a Catholic, I categorized the sins in my
life as either venial sin or mortal sin. Venial sin, according
to the Baltimore Catechism, is a less serious offense against
the law of God which does not deprive the soul of sanctifying
grace (a special grace I received at the time of my baptism as
an infant that allowed me the privilege of going to heaven).
Some examples of venial sins would be lying, stealing small
items, cheating, gossiping, using vulgar language, arguing,
and missing Mass on Sunday. Any venial sins I committed
could be pardoned, even without confessing them to a priest.
As I took stock of my sinful life, I felt most of the sins I had
committed were venial sins.

I was always warned to be on my guard against the capital sins which are the source of all other sins and could
lead me to committing "mortal sins." The capital sins were
identified as pride, lust, anger, gluttony, envy, and laziness.
I was taught that mortal sin was a grievous offense against
the law of God which deprived the soul of sanctifying grace.
A sin became mortal when an action, thought, or desire was
considered seriously wrong and the sinner gave full con-

sent to it. Several examples of mortal sins would be drunkenness, adultery, and murder.

I desired to be reconciled with God. I knew my sins had separated me from God. I had lived my life as a Catholic under the law. From Romans 3:23 I realized that the smallest sin I had committed made me fall short of God's acceptance. In James 2:10 I read that if a person claims to keep the whole law and yet violates one of its commandments he is guilty of breaking all the commandments. James said it this way, "For whoever shall keep the whole law, and yet stumble in one point, he is guilty of all" (James 2:10).

God is pure and holy and no sin can ever be allowed in His holy presence:

> Righteousness and justice are the foundation of His throne (Psalm 97:2).

> But your iniquities have separated you from your God; And your sins have hidden His face from you, So that He will not hear (Isaiah 59:2).

I learned from Bible classes that it was impossible to save myself, either through earned merits, special graces, or the law. From Romans 3:20 I was able to grasp the meaning of God's message when He said, "Therefore by the deeds of the law no flesh will be justified in His sight, for by the law is the knowledge of sin."

I was taught that baptism brought me into Jesus and presented me in a righteous state before God. Other than the Eucharist, baptism is one of the most important teachings of Roman Catholicism. The Catholic Church has always emphasized the importance of baptism and has always taken the greatest care that no child departed from this world without receiving this sacrament. The beginning of my natural life took place at birth, but the beginning of my spiritual life took place at my baptism. Throughout the years I studied Roman Catholicism I believed that baptism as an infant united me with God and His church. Being baptized brought forgiveness of all my sins, especially original sin. This is the sin I supposedly inherited from my first parents, Adam and Eve. Before my baptism, my parents were to choose the name of a saint for me to imitate and to have for a protector throughout my life. As an infant, I could not believe, repent, or confess my sins, so a godparent, or sponsor, was chosen to make this commitment for me.

As I read John's account of Nicodemus' conversation with Jesus about the kingdom of God I comprehended the concept of being born again. I knew that as a baby I had not become a new creature in Christ. I had not been born again as Jesus directed.

> There was a man of the Pharisees named Nicodemus, a ruler of the Jews. This man came to Jesus by night and said to Him, "Rabbi, we know that You are a teacher come from God; for no one can do these signs that You do unless God is with him." Jesus answered and said to him, "Most assuredly, I say to you, unless one is born again, he cannot see the kingdom of God." Nicodemus said to Him, "How can a man be born when he is old? Can he enter a second time into his mother's womb and be born?" Jesus answered, "Most assuredly, I say to you, unless one is born of water and the Spirit, he cannot enter the kingdom of God. That which is born of the flesh is flesh, and that which is born of the Spirit is spirit" (John 3:1-6).

Jesus had pointed out the dissimilarity in the two births. That which is born of the flesh produces a sinful, corruptible nature under the sentence of death and the influence of Satan. That which is born of the Spirit produces a new birth with a sinless, righteous, and divine nature.

My baptism as an infant was invalid before God because only believers could be baptized as Scripture taught. I could not believe, repent, or confess my sins as a baby. In Ezekiel 18:20, God says that children are innocent and are not in a lost condition:

The soul who sins shall die. The son shall not bear the guilt of the father, nor the father bear the guilt of the son. The righteousness of the righteous shall be upon himself, and the wickedness of the wicked shall be upon himself.

The new birth was a necessity for me to be saved and to enjoy a right relationship with God. I was sorry for my sins and my past life. Most of all, I was sorry that Jesus had to die on the cross for sins that were mine and mine alone. I was willing to surrender my total life to God — my mind, my heart, and my will — not only as a living sacrifice to God but also as a grateful response to Jesus who paid it all.

On October 4, 1972, I confessed openly my faith and my desire to be born again as Timothy did (1 Timothy 6:12) and as the Ethiopian nobleman did (Acts 8:37). I rejoiced in the moment when I died to my past and was buried with Christ in the waters of baptism, to rise as a new creature. I was changed from a servant of sin into a servant of righteousness (Romans 6:17-18).

I was no longer lost, for I have been saved from my own self-righteousness. I am no longer a servant of Satan but a child of God (John 8:44; Romans 8:16-17). I have become united with the people of God (1 Peter 2:9-10). I have been delivered out of darkness and transported into the kingdom of God's dear Son (Colossians 1:3).

Faith started the salvation process; the power of the Word of God took hold of my mind and began to change my thinking and purpose of life. Baptism changed my relationship and allowed me the right of eternal happiness with God. I have never regretted taking that walk in faith to become one with Christ in my burial with Him through baptism. Daily I open my heart and my mind to God's Word. I find my hope and strength in the assurance God has given me in His revealed and inspired Word as I stand on His promises.

I have discovered that the Christian life is not a bed of roses, for my earthly troubles did not cease the moment I accepted Christ and He added me to His church (Acts 2:47). In certain ways my troubles have increased because of the responsibility I have committed myself to in sharing the Gospel with others — especially my family. I have also experienced great joy, as in seeing my dear mother, at the age of 78, added to God's family as she too gave her life to Him in the waters of baptism.

The great difference now is that I have Jesus as my sole advocate, and He teaches and comforts me daily through the Word. Jesus has been the only answer to my soul's need for spiritual nourishment and abundant life.

Jesus promised in Matthew 16:18-19 that He would build His church and nothing would ever prevail against it — no denomination or creed. He has kept both promises. He built His church, and His church is still in the world today.

For years I had walked in a forest of entangled doctrines and misguided paths to truth, searching for an illumination from the darkness of uncertainty and man-made directions. I have found the opening to peace and joy I knew was available. God's illumination through His Word has changed the path I now travel toward eternity. I have found in the arms of Jesus that for which I have always searched. His ways, His truths, and His peace have become my bread of life!

Scripture and Tradition — The Heart of the Matter

ৣৣৣ

"The Bible will tell you who you are, where you are going, and how you will get there." Ever since these words were planted in my mind and my heart, I have had an unquenchable desire for an in-depth knowledge of the Bible's contents and an understanding of its truths.

The history of mankind reveals a continuing search for truth in the natural world as well as in the realm of religion. As a former Roman Catholic, I adhered to a religion established almost entirely on tradition. I am convinced that I would still be searching for godly truths revealed through men's teachings today had I not investigated the Word of God:

> O LORD, I know the way of man is not in himself; It is not in man who walks to direct his own steps (Jeremiah 10:23).

> There is a way that seems right to a man, But its end is the way of death (Proverbs 16:25).

Throughout the ages, the Bible has proved itself to be a Book of high spiritual potency and unerring truths. I have read many political speeches where kings and rulers alike, even Jesus, drew inner strength and direction from the messages contained in God's Word. Time and again, the Bible has demonstrated to me a mysterious power to change people's lives, ennoble the human spirit, enrich the mind, enlarge the vision, and transform the natural man from a carnal being into a spiritual fortress of strength against Satan and his evil forces.

As strange as the paradox may seem, I honored every word that was uttered at Mass from God's holy Word, yet I knew nothing about God's plan for my salvation as revealed in His Word.

I was told that as a Catholic I could derive historical knowledge about Jesus, His life, His teachings, and the church He established through the books of the Bible. I remember being taught that besides being reliable historical records, the books of the Bible are God's inspired word, written by men with the direct assistance of God's Holy Spirit.

Since the publication of my first book, *A Change of Habit*, I have received considerable correspondence from Catholics throughout the United States, Canada, and abroad. Several of these letters were from priests and nuns. The following comment reveals the reasons why I had a difficult time as a Roman Catholic accepting the Bible as my only authority:

> From all of the teaching you have received concerning biblical knowledge, you should be aware of the Catholic Church's position on tradition. The Church maintains its position that some mistakes have crept into the copies and translations of the Bible. The Church believes that not all truths have been revealed to us by God, but are found in Divine Tradition. There are many teachings that were taught by the Apostles which were given to the Church only by word of mouth. They were put in writing by the Fathers of the Church and passed on from one generation to

another. Tradition is considered the highest authority in the Catholic Church today.

As I have grown toward maturity in my knowledge of God's Word, my faith is built on nothing less than the infallibility of the Bible, revealed for my learning and salvation. Unwritten or oral tradition necessitates continued inspiration. No one with whom I have spoken in the Catholic Church can prove to me that unwritten tradition was ever taught by inspired apostles or practiced by churches of the first century by the authority of any apostle.

The Word of God is the only real authority we have:

> All Scripture is given by inspiration of God, and is profitable for doctrine, for reproof, for correction, for instruction in righteousness, that the man of God may be complete, thoroughly equipped for every good work (2 Timothy 3:16-17).

Since these verses tell me that scriptures are inspired and furnish me completely for every good work, it follows that unwritten traditions cannot reveal any duty which I have to God or man and are not essential to my salvation. These inspired words declare that the scriptures of God teach, train, inspire, guide, and make the man of God perfect in the knowledge of God's will as revealed through Jesus and His apostles.

In the Old Testament, God warned the people not to add to or take from scriptures those words which He revealed and inspired the writers to pen:

> "You shall not add to the word which I command you, nor take from it, that you may keep the commandments of the LORD your God which I command you" (Deuteronomy 4:2).

> To the law and to the testimony! If they do not speak according to this word, it is because there is no light in them (Isaiah 8:20).

Jesus frequently condemned following tradition and warned His disciples that following the teachings of men makes the Word of God of no effect. He said that honoring human traditions as doctrine make worship to His Father unacceptable:

> He answered and said to them, "Why do you also transgress the commandment of God because of your tradition? ... Thus you have made the commandment of God of no effect by your tradition. Hypocrites! Well did Isaiah prophesy about you, saying: 'These people draw near to Me with their mouth, And honor Me with their lips, But their heart is far from Me. And in vain they worship Me, Teaching as doctrines the commandments of men' " (Matthew 15:3, 6-9).

> He said to them, "All too well you reject the commandment of God, that you may keep your tradition ... making the word of God of no effect through your tradition which you have handed down. And many such things you do" (Mark 7:9, 13).

As I understand these passages, Jesus is telling me that human tradition keeps the Word of His Father from accomplishing its purpose in the lives of those He created. When men mix their human traditions with the laws of God, these traditions become unacceptable before His throne.

Paul warned the followers of Jesus about accepting tradition as their rule of faith and final authority:

> Beware lest anyone cheat you through philosophy and empty deceit, according to the tradition of men, according to the basic principles of the world, and not according to Christ (Colossians 2:8).

Paul also cautions that human reasoning is vain and deceptive. The Holy Spirit, who inspired and revealed every scripture that was written for mankind's learning, recognized that no salvation could come to mankind through human philosophies, worldly experiences, history, traditions, or wisdom of men.

I learned in my Catholic training a statement from Augustine, one of the early leaders in the Church: "Thou hast made us for Thyself, O Lord, and our hearts shall ever be restless, until they rest in Thee."

The word "heart" as it is used in Scripture, is identified as the seat of life, all human reasoning, and affection. In this context the heart refers to our mind, soul, strength, and spirit as well as one's entire emotional nature and understanding.

The psalmist David understood the condition of his own heart. He knew that God tries the heart, and in this penitent prayer David petitioned God:

> Create in me a clean heart, O God, And renew a steadfast spirit within me ... The sacrifices of God are a broken spirit, A broken and a contrite heart — These, O God, You will not despise (Psalm 51:10, 17).

In 1 Samuel and Jeremiah, God tells us how He sees the human heart:

> But the LORD said to Samuel, "Do not look at his appearance or at the height of his stature, because I have refused him. For the Lord does not see as man sees; for man looks at the outward appearance, but the LORD looks at the heart" (1 Samuel 16:7).

> The heart is deceitful above all things, And desperately wicked; Who can know it? (Jeremiah 17:9).

In Proverbs God tells us what we are to do with our heart. He says, "Keep your heart with all diligence, For out of it spring the issues of life" (Proverbs 4:23).

Spiritual discovery through the teachings of God's Word has anchored me in Christ's wisdom and Christ's philosophy. I have chosen Christ alone as my way of righteousness. My heart is wicked, vain, and deceitful. God says that Christ must be the source, the substance and the truth of every doctrine I believe and accept. My destiny is everlasting death unless I accept His teachings.

The ecclesiastic authorities in the Roman Catholic Church truly believe they have found the way to truth and eternal happiness. To assure that my theological background was well-grounded in the doctrines of the Catholic Church and church history, I was taught a course in Bible history during my early training in the convent. The ecclesiastic authorities in Rome strongly emphasized in their teachings the doctrine that "the Catholic Church is the mother of the Bible."

The Catholic Church declared that it derived all of its teaching authority from those doctrines passed on to them from Christ. The First Vatican Council which occurred in 1870 reaffirmed this by stating that the Church holds the books of both the Old and New Testaments as sacred and canonical, not because, having been composed by human industry, they were afterwards approved by her authority, not merely because they contain revelation without error, but because having been without error, they were written under the inspiration of the Holy Spirit and they have God as their Author.[1]

The Roman Catholic Church would have us believe that the Bible is difficult to understand, even among Bible scholars. To interpret the Bible, those in authority believe it is not only necessary to understand the languages in which the Bible was written but also necessary to understand the meanings that the words of the Bible had at the time they were written. Proclaiming to be the guardian and infallible interpreter of the Bible, the Catholic Church teaches that God's Holy Spirit gives them the right to speak for Him through direct succession of the apostles.

In John 16:13, I read where Jesus promised to send the Spirit to guide the apostles into all truth. Earlier, Jesus confirmed this power of Scripture when He proclaimed: "You search the Scriptures, for in them you think you have eternal life; and these are they which testify of Me" (John 5:39).

In Ephesians 3, Paul acknowledges Christ's revelation to him and the instruction he has been given for his ministry. But he assures the Ephesian Christians that they also are able to understand the "mysteries" revealed to the apostles and prophets because of the Holy Spirit who will guide them.

[I]f indeed you have heard of the dispensation of the grace of God which was given to me for you, how that by revelation He made known to me the mystery (as I have briefly written already, by which, when you read, you may understand my knowledge in the mystery of Christ), which in other ages was not made known to the sons of men, as it has now been revealed by the Spirit to His holy apostles and prophets (Ephesians 3:2-5).

I had always felt so inadequate in my understanding of Scripture. I believed every interpretation the Catholic Church professed as truth, not knowing or realizing that most of their doctrines were unwritten traditions. Many former Catholics who are now saved have conveyed similar beliefs. Another former nun wrote me the following poignant letter:

Joanne,

I just want you to know that I could relate to excerpts from your book, especially when you commented on discovering truths in the Bible that were not based on the traditions you had professed as a Catholic.

I have much in common with you, as I too entered a convent and remained there for nine years. I entered right after high school and tried to learn all that was required of me. I entered right before Vatican II had convened in 1962. I wasn't happy and I tried to leave several times, but the pressure to stay was enormous. I finally "ran away" in May of 1969. I was told I was going to hell as I entered a world carrying tons of guilt and fear with me. I eventually received my dispensation from Rome. I tried to make up for my past "sin" by being a good Catholic. But in my heart I felt I had committed the "unpardonable sin" of turning away from God because I had rejected my vocation and abandoned my vows.

Finally, in September 1970, I became "born again" and my eyes are now opened to the truths available to me in God's Word. I had no idea I was lost, nor did I realize God had a plan for me, here and in eternity. I have been angry that the Catholic Church has kept the study of God's Word away from its people. Hopefully, many Catholics will come to know the truth, and it will make them as free as you and I have become in His Kingdom. It has been an incredible journey, but now, we are both on the right road to heaven!

Sue

What an awesome experience it is to discover that you are loved by Jesus — no matter the circumstances of your life! What an incredible relief it is when you discover the assurance of this in His Word. What a tremendous burden is lifted when you repent of your sins and become one with Jesus in the waters of baptism! Like Sue, I thought I had covered all the bases in keeping the law until I learned the difference between tradition and divine inspiration of God's Word.

Not once in all the years I attended both parochial grammar school and high school can I recall a nun or a priest teaching the students how to defend Catholic doctrine through the use of Scripture. When I was shown Catholic doctrines that were unfounded scripturally, I felt threatened because of my ignorance of the Bible. Since I had never openly questioned my religion, I was confounded because of my lack of defense for my Catholic beliefs. I had blindly accepted the official teachings of Roman Catholicism without examining the Bible for myself.

I asked myself this question as a small child, "What does God want me to do when I grow up?" I have been given many answers throughout my life and have taken many side roads to follow those answers, but none seemed to satisfy me until I met Jesus through His Word. Jesus knocked on the door of my heart with these words from John 14:6: "I am the way, the truth, and the life."

Since Jesus said He was the "truth," I knew the truth I was searching for could be found in Him. My knowledge of Him had become obscured by the twisting of teachings I had learned about Him as a Catholic. Thus, I aspired to know all I could about Him and His Father through the Bible.

I started to read in earnest, but my knowledge about how to study the Bible was extremely limited. I was grateful I could distinguish between the Old and New Testaments. Yet, unfamiliar phraseology and confusing passages seemed completely beyond my understanding. Because I had always seen the Bible used as a tool of magisterium upon the altar at church, I expected it to be a profound theological treatise, weighed down with a multitude of statements from ecclesiastical authorities. I had a difficult time conceptualizing the scriptures as a fabulous mine of spiritual riches waiting for me to unearth them.

In reading, studying, and investigating the various books of the Bible, I began to see how the Bible was God's way of unveiling the truth for me — truth I would not know without His sharing it with me. God allowed me to see the truth about my past history, my present condition, and my future. Through Scripture, God revealed Himself and His Son. He also explained my uniqueness, my sinfulness and my relationship to Him. The Bible became God's personal letter to me.

The focal point of both the Old and New Testament was to bring me to Jesus. I saw that God had a plan for each group of people throughout history. In the Old Testament, I read how God communicated to His people through two earlier periods of time — the Patriarchal Age and the Mosaic Age. In this current and last age — the Christian Age — God communicates with His people through Christ and the apostles and their inspired writings.

The Patriarchal Age begins with the story of creation, the first people, the first children, and the first sin. Here I read how God provided sacrifice for sin. This period of time began with Adam and ended with the giving of the Mosaic Law to Moses on Mt. Sinai. During this period of time there was no church, no temple, and no written system of laws. God spoke directly to the Patriarchs of the families (such as Abraham, Isaac, Jacob and Joseph) through visions, dreams, and angels. As people multiplied on the earth, they became exceedingly wicked, and because they would not repent they were destroyed by a great flood, except for eight people who believed and obeyed God. The Patriarchal Age ends with the deliverance of God's people from Egyptian slavery.

The second period of communication between God and His people is known as the Mosaic Age. This period lasted for about 1500 years. During this period there was the tabernacle and later the temple at the center of worship to God. There was also an elaborate system of laws centered around the Ten Commandments. To carry out the extensive system of sacrifices and intercessions, there was a carefully regulated priesthood. Under Moses' direction, God delivered His chosen people, the Israelites, out of bondage in Egypt. Unbelief on the part of many Israelites brought heartaches and misery to their tribes, which caused God's people to wander in the wilderness 40 years before reaching the Promised Land.

There are many great stories from the Mosaic Age. I read about the kings of Israel and the division of the kingdom under their reign. There were stories about the prophets sent by God who warned the people and foretold the coming of the Savior. The Mosaic Age ended with the life, death, burial, and resurrection of our Savior, Jesus.

Finally, I read about the Christian Age and the establishment of Christ's church. This age has lasted nearly 2000 years. It will continue in effect until Christ returns to announce the end of time and the judgment. The temple was replaced by the church, which includes all Christians. The law of Moses (including the Ten Commandments) was replaced by the greater law of liberty, the law of Christ. Through the inspirational writings of the gospel accounts of Matthew, Mark, Luke, and John and the epistles of Peter, Paul, James, and Jude, the Holy Spirit of God gave complete revelation for God's people today.

In reading the Bible, I see God as the great communicator. He made His will known to and through the Old Testament prophets. He guided Jesus and inspired the apostles. The book of Acts records several instances of detailed guidance on the message of salvation — to the Ethiopian eunuch (Acts 8:26, 29) and Peter when he is told to accept the invitation to teach Cornelius and his family (Acts 10:1-48). Moreover, Scripture contains explicit promises of divine guidance that help me to know God's plan for my actions. In Psalm 32:8 God tells David: "I will instruct you and teach you in the way you should go; I will guide you with My eye." Other scriptures also declare this to be true:

> Good and upright is the LORD; Therefore He teaches sinners in the way. The humble He guides in justice, And the humble He teaches His way ... Who is the man that fears the LORD? Him shall He teach in the way He chooses (Psalm 25:8-9, 12).

> In all your ways acknowledge Him, And He shall direct your paths (Proverbs 3:6).

One of the sermons on Bible history that left an impression on me referred to the division of the Old and New Testaments in scripture. I recall hearing the preacher say, "The Old Testament is the New Testament concealed; the New Testament is the Old Testament revealed."

The Old Testament was preparatory, temporary, and limited. The New Testament is complete, eternal, and universal. The New Testament was prophesied by Isaiah when he spoke of the days when the new law would go forth from Jerusalem:

> Now it shall come to pass in the latter days That the mountain of the LORD'S house Shall be established on

the top of the mountains, And shall be exalted above the hills; And all nations shall flow to it. Many people shall come and say, "Come, and let us go up to the mountain of the LORD, To the house of the God of Jacob; He will teach us His ways, And we shall walk in His paths." For out of Zion shall go forth the law, And the word of the LORD from Jerusalem (Isaiah 2:2-3).

Jeremiah promised a new covenant writing:

"Behold, the days are coming, says the LORD, when I will make a new covenant with the house of Israel and with the house of Judah — not according to the covenant that I made with their fathers in the day that I took them by the hand to lead them out of the land of Egypt, My covenant which they broke, though I was a husband to them, says the LORD. But this is the covenant that I will make with the house of Israel after those days, says the LORD: I will put My law in their minds, and write it on their hearts; and I will be their God, and they shall be My people" (Jeremiah 31:31-33).

Paul declared that the law was added until the seed (Christ) would come:

What purpose then does the law serve? It was added because of transgressions, till the Seed should come to whom the promise was made" (Galatians 3:19).

When Jesus came, He said His coming was to fulfill the law and the prophets. The Old Testament was of a temporary nature, designed to show men their need of a Savior: "Do not think that I came to destroy the Law or the Prophets. I did not come to destroy but to fulfill" (Matthew 5:17).

The death of Jesus marked the end of the old covenant and the beginning of the new covenant. The Old Testament covered thousands of years, and the New Testament about a century. Yet, that century was the most important in the history of mankind. It was during those years that Jesus was born, conducted His public ministry, was crucified, and was resurrected. Messianic prophecy was fulfilled, and God's plan of salvation was accomplished. The birth, the establishment, and the initial expansion of the church also occurred in that century.

The 27 books of the New Testament are filled with intense drama, inspired teaching, and practical instruction. According to the New Testament itself, they originated in the mind of God, came to us by divine inspiration, and were kept from error through the ministry of the Holy Spirit:

> All Scripture is given by inspiration of God, and is profitable for doctrine, for reproof, for correction, for instruction in righteousness, that the man of God may be complete, thoroughly equipped for every good work (2 Timothy 3:16-17).

The word "testament" means "covenant" or "agreement." The New Testament tells of a new relationship between God and man — a new way of knowing God and communicating with Him. The old covenant was made with the Jewish nation. The Jewish background of the New Testament was important because Christianity was born in a Jewish environment. Christianity was rooted in what God had already made known to His people through the Old Testament. The new covenant was made with people of every nation who accepted by faith the salvation offered them through Jesus Christ.

The books of the New Testament are not arranged in the order in which they were written, but are placed in four literary groupings:

> Gospels — Four biographies of Jesus Christ
> Book of Acts — The history of the early church
> Letters (Epistles) to the churches — Twenty-one
>   letters defining a Christian's belief and practice
> Revelation — Visions given to John

It was exciting for me to finally become knowledgeable of the background of this great book. The more I read, the more I wanted to know. And this desire continues to this very day. In my enthusiasm to share what I had learned, I initiated conversations which would include my new-found treasure, the Bible. The following response was made by many of my Catholic friends and relatives: "The Bible has been revised and rewritten in so many different languages since the time of Christ, that much of its content could be flawed through human error."

When I first heard this criticism, I decided to study and research on the original writings of the Bible. The initial language of the books of the New Testament was written in Koine Greek, the common language of the Greco-Roman world at that time. As the Gospel spread to far-off places, a demand for different translations was created: for Syria, the Syriac translation; for Egypt, the Coptic versions; and for the area of Africa that had once been Carthage, the Gospel was written in Latin. I remember explaining to my father the difference between translation and transmission when he questioned the authenticity of its writers. I described this concept by relating to my mother's ability to translate words from the Russian language into English. There were words in Russian that could not be translated into English, and a synonym had to be used. As the Bible has had many translations throughout the course of history, the transmission from God would always remain the same. God confirmed this in His Word when He spoke through Isaiah saying:

> So shall My word be that goes forth from My mouth;
> It shall not return to Me void, But it shall accomplish
> what I please, And it shall prosper in the thing for
> which I sent it (Isaiah 55:11).

The manuscript evidence supporting the Bible's accuracy is overwhelming. There are more than 5,500 Greek manuscripts of the New Testament and more than 10,000 manuscripts of the Latin Vulgate version translated by Jerome in A.D. 386. These manuscripts were hand copied through a laborious and time-consuming process. The Latin Vulgate Bible became the official version of the Roman Catholic Church and remains so until this day. The Roman Catholic Bible in English is actually a translation of a translation, not a translation from the original manuscripts as are others.

Throughout my research, I have been amazed to read how God has been able to preserve His Word through the recordings of men in different periods of time. In the spring of 1947, in the Judean wilderness, near the northwestern corner of the Dead Sea, a Bedouin shepherd was looking for his lost sheep. He happened to come upon an opening in a cave and threw a stone inside. He heard the cracking of a jar and went in to investigate. There he discovered several clay jars. Inside these jars were ancient manuscripts that have come to be known as the "Dead Sea Scrolls."

This discovery of ancient biblical manuscripts in Hebrew and Aramaic, written before A.D. 70, contained fragments of every Old Testament Book except Esther. While these manuscripts alone can neither prove nor disprove the inspiration of the Bible, they clearly indicate that a community of Jews who lived more than 19 centuries ago possessed a library of sacred writings which, in all essential details, is the same as the Bible which we have regarded as authoritative.

Many Catholics with whom I have shared scripture taken from the Old Testament denounce many of the Bible's stories as mere fiction. One individual wrote me saying:

> How could you believe the story of the flood when it has never been authenticated? And what about the story of Jonah? How could someone live in the belly of a whale for three days and nights? Don't you think these stories are a bit farfetched?

The deciding difference in this man's belief and my own is the fact that I believe that all Scripture has been God-breathed. I don't believe I have the right to pick and choose those I want to believe. In Hebrews 6:18 the writer tells us "it is impossible for God to lie."

The Bible makes some very strong claims concerning its divine source of authorship, inspiration, and content. It repeatedly confirms the fact that God is both the architect and author. These facts are emphasized by the following passages:

> [K]nowing this first, that no prophecy of Scripture is of any private interpretation, for prophecy never came by the will of man, but holy men of God spoke as they were moved by the Holy Spirit (2 Peter 1:20-21).

> "Heaven and earth will pass away, but My words will by no means pass away" (Matthew 24:35).

> For whatever things were written before were written for our learning, that we through the patience and comfort of the Scriptures might have hope (Romans 15:4).

Paul claimed his message came from God:

> But I make known to you, brethren, that the gospel which was preached by me is not according to man. For I neither received it from man, nor was I taught it, but it came through the revelation of Jesus Christ (Galatians 1:11-12).

I would have loved to have lived during the time Jesus walked this earth. What a privilege it would have been to hear the words He spoke directly.

Traditionally, word of mouth and memorization by rote were the acceptable means of communication during this period in history. As time passed, the need to record and evaluate the historical teachings and the words of Jesus became a necessity. Many heretical sects were producing corrupt teachings, and ruthless persecutions were being unleashed against the church. Some writings were considered by all to have been inspired, while others were regarded more highly by some groups of Christians than others. There was a need to determine which writings could be trusted. Thus, the formation of the biblical canon began at the Council of Nicea in A.D. 325. Fraudulent writings during the second century and persecution under Diocletian's reign of terror in the fourth century spurred the completion of the formal ratification of the 27 books of the New Testament canon under the Emperor Constantine. Christianity became the national religion during the reign of Constantine. He commissioned Eusebius to convene a council to determine which books were to be placed in the canon. The word "canon" is derived from the Greek word for "reed" and means "a cane, rule or measuring rod." This word is now used to mean a list of writings divinely inspired in both the Old and New Testaments.

This historical process of determining which books met the canonical requirements was not finalized overnight but over many centuries. The dilemma that faced the church was the question of which books were the authoritative Word of God. Many books were forgeries or contained counterfeit scriptures. Therefore, specific rules were adopted for determining which writings met the requirements for being included in the sacred canon. The 66 books that were chosen met the following strict standards:

1. Does the book possess a definite prophetic and inspirational quality; does it manifest a clear "Thus saith the Lord?"

2. Was the book written by a reputable prophet, authored by an apostle, or a contemporary intimately associated with an apostle?

3. Was the book accepted, collected, preserved, distributed, and read by God's people either in the Old Testament period or New Testament period?

4. Do its contents and message harmonize with the standards of sound biblical teaching? Many of the false writings contained an abundance of fanciful legends, factual inaccuracies, and doctrinal heresies.

5. Does it possess a dynamic, life-transforming power which has a universal impact upon men?

6. Was it endorsed and accepted by successive generations of believers, such as the early church fathers? In other words, there seemed to be a consistent, prevailing witness of the overwhelming majority of the church concerning a book's divine inspiration.[2]

Realizing the significance of the above criteria for canonical status is very important. In comparing the Bible with the Catholic Bible, I observed that seven books had been added to the Old Testament canon by the Catholic Church — Tobit, Judith, 1 Maccabees, 2 Maccabees, Wisdom, Sirach, and Baruch. A former Catholic priest explained to me that these seven books were known as "Apocryphal Books." Other apocryphal writings added to the Catholic Bible are the books of 1 and 2 Esdras, Susanna, Bell and the Dragon, additions to the book of Esther, the letter of Jeremiah, and the Prayer of Azariah and the Song of the Three Young Men. These are regarded as inspired scripture in the Catholic Church. I was also surprised to learn that these apocryphal books were not a part of the Old Testament of Jesus and the early church. The three-fold division of the Old Testament — the Law, the Prophets, and the Writings — are still used in Hebrew Bibles and Jewish versions of the Old Testament. The apocryphal books are not included in this grouping. Although the Apocrypha was known to Jesus and His disciples, they never quoted from these texts as authoritative Scripture. Most non-Catholic churches reject the Apocrypha as inspired Scripture for the following reasons:

1. The apocryphal books were not a part of the testament of Jesus and the early church.

2. Ancient Jewish writers who used the Greek Bible were acquainted with the Apocryhpha but never quote it in Scripture.

3. Church Fathers who were familiar with the Hebrew canon clearly distinguish between canonical and Apocryphal writings.

4. The apocryphal books were never declared to be authoritative Scripture until the Council of Trent convened in 1546.

5. Most readers believe that the apocryphal books represent a lower level of writing than that of the canonical scriptures. They contain numerous historical and geographical inaccuracies and do not have the prophetic spirit that is evident in the canonical scriptures.[3]

Some churches, such as the Reformed Church and the Anglican Church, take a mediating position on the books of the Apocrypha and consider them worthwhile reading for example of life and instruction of manners, yet they do not adhere to any of their doctrine.

In John 1:1 we read, "In the beginning was the Word, and the Word was with God, and the Word was God." As the curtain rises on the drama of life, two are already on stage, God and the Word. Each of us has a scene in this great drama. However, in order to understand the script, each of us must be able to know the writer's intentions and then be able to communicate the message he conveys to the audience.

The next time you pick up a Bible consider its usage with this thought in mind:

God gave me the Bible because He wants me to know about Him. In the script He has written for me, God wants me to become united with Him, and He wants my personal character to become transformed into His likeness. By obeying every direction God has given me in His Word, I will grow into acting like Him, and I will be able to share this message with the world.

One of the greatest experiences of my life has been the exciting, first-hand study I have been able to do in God's Word. As John wrote: "But the anointing which you have received from Him abides in you, and you do not need that anyone teach you" (1 John 2:27).

I visited the invalid husband of a co-teacher over a 13-year period. I enjoyed talking to him about God, praying with him, and leaving little tracts about the Bible for him to study. While visiting him one evening, he blurted out: "Joanne, I need to be baptized. Can you provide someone in your church to immerse me for the remission of my sins?" I asked him how he came to this conclusion, as it had been more than a year since I had last visited with him. His response was:

> For over a year now, I have read the tracts you have given me, and I have read the scriptures they referred to when we studied different subjects. In reading the scriptures for myself, there was only one logical conclusion I could come to, and that was the importance of baptism in the sight of God.

His ability to first examine various facts and then draw a logical conclusion from them helped his inductive reasoning process. I, myself, learned to study the Bible from deductive reasoning. I would start with a statement of doctrine which I would want to prove from evidence in the Bible. Then, I would take the scriptures I would find as evidence that might or might not prove my doctrine to be scriptural. I was making Scripture fit my preconceived ideas.

Let me suggest some practical ways that might be of help in your own pursuit of Bible study:

1. Present your heart before the throne of God in repentance, humble submission, and faith in His Word.

2. Choose a passage from one of the books in the Old or New Testament to meditate on to nourish and uplift your soul. I have found that Psalms encourages me toward a deeper faith and trust in God.

3. Read this passage over and over until like the rain, it saturates your thirsty soul.

4. Look for God's message for you that day. This may include a promise, a command or a timeless principle.

5. Draw a practical application from this message.

6. Keep a spiritual diary, and refer to it as often as you can during the day.

7. Thank God for His grace to persevere in the knowledge and obedience to His Word.

One of the most revered messages I have received from the study of God's Word is incorporated in these special words from Matthew 6:33: "But seek first the kingdom of God and His righteousness, and all these things shall be added to you."

Jesus has become my way, my truth, and my life as I journey through this life with God's revelation for me — the Bible.

Biblical Authority – Who Has the Power?

✦

Throughout my childhood and young adult life, I heard repeated warnings concerning dangers threatening the authority of the pope in Rome and the ecclesiastical authority of the Roman Catholic Church worldwide. Many of these dangers were of an internal nature, resulting from the questioning of dissident Catholics. Other dangers arose from various religious groups protesting the political control of the Vatican throughout the world. The threat of these persuasive influences became very real after the second Vatican Council, causing the powers in Rome to expend vast amounts of energy substantiating its biblical authority. Another device used to unite these opposing forces was the development of the ecumenical movement, designed to bring about more uniformity of belief among the various churches worldwide. The word "ecumenical" means "general or worldwide." Those churches not professing Catholic beliefs were considered to be "separated brethren."

With all these dangers, my greatest concern has always been for the proclamation of truth and the preservation of the true church established by Jesus Christ. Because of these concerns, I investigated the teachings of Roman Catholicism regarding its claims on biblical authority and compared them with the scriptural teachings of the apostles.

Catholic Claim for Papal Authority

According to the doctrine I learned and taught as a Catholic nun, the Roman Catholic Church traces itself back to Christ's statement to Peter, "[Y]ou are Peter, and on this rock I will build My church, and the gates of Hades shall not prevail against it" (Matthew 16:18). Peter was considered by Catholics to be the prince of the apostles, and from him followed an unbroken succession of Roman Catholic popes.

The first Vatican Council (1869-1870) confirmed this linkage as a doctrine of faith. The Council was called during a time of persecution of the Roman Catholic Church, when the papacy was not at the height of its power and prestige. Hoping to restore its authority and image, the Council came up with the following definition of infallibility:

> The Roman Pontiff, when he speaks *ex cathedra*, that is, when in the discharge of the office of pastor and doctor of all Christians, by virtue of his supreme apostolic authority he defines a doctrine regarding faith or morals to be held by the universal Church, by the divine assistance promised to him in blessed Peter, is possessed of that infallibility with which the divine Redeemer willed that his Church should be endowed for defining doctrine regarding faith and morals: and therefore such definitions are irreformable of themselves and not from the consent of the Church.[4]

The Council stated clearly that the pope is gifted with infallibility and that his decisions are unchangeable. The Council taught that in order for a statement of a pope to be considered infallible, his statement must meet the following conditions:

1. His teaching must concern the teachings of the

Gospels (necessary for salvation); it must be a question of faith or morals.

2. He must address the entire Christian community and not just a part of it.

3. He must explicitly state that what he is saying is binding, to be believed by all.

4. He must speak "ex cathedra," i.e., as official teacher of the entire church.[5]

Despite attempts by some to offer a qualified interpretation of this pronouncement, the principle of papal authority was upheld and reaffirmed forcefully by the Second Vatican Council:

> The college or body of bishops has no authority unless it is simultaneously conceived of in terms of its head, the Roman Pontiff, Peter's successor, and without any lessening of his power of primacy over all, pastors as well as the general faithful. For in virtue of his office, that is, as Vicar of Christ and pastor of the whole Church, the Roman Pontiff has full, supreme, and universal power over the Church. And he can always exercise this power freely.[6]

According to the standards of Vatican I, only two of the pope's teachings in recent times have been considered infallible definitions of Christian faith: the doctrine of the Immaculate Conception of Mary (proclaimed in 1854) and the doctrine of the Assumption of Mary into heaven (proclaimed in 1950).

To justify and defend the dogma of infallibility, I was taught that Christ left an authority who would speak with an infallible voice. This authority was the pope in Rome. Anyone who disagreed with the pope was considered an anathema (an abomination to the Lord and a heretic). The entire system of Catholicism, based on the primacy of the pope, left no opening for inquiring minds. The magesterium (or teaching authority) of the pope was infallible and irrefutable when a dogma was declared on matters of faith or morals. I was taught to believe that Christ wished His church to submit and revere the pope as His vicar on earth.

I recall as a child hearing my mother question the infallibility of the pope. She saw him as a human being without the ability to be absolute on anything regarding one's faith. It was plainly evident that I too needed to give further examination to this teaching. I questioned, "How can the cardinals (who are fallible human beings) vote on the selection of another fallible human, who will become infallible?"

During my study of church history, I recall reading a statement of one of the predecessors of the present pope, Pope Gregory the Great. He had rejected the title of Universal Bishop in A.D. 595. He quoted from Matthew 23:9-12 to prove that such a title was blasphemous:

> Do not call anyone on earth your father; for One is your Father, He who is in heaven. And do not be called teachers; for One is your Teacher, the Christ. But he who is greatest among you shall be your servant. And whoever exalts himself will be humbled, and he who humbles himself will be exalted (Matthew 23:9-12).[7]

Attwater's Catholic Dictionary states, "Peter was the first pope and he was upon the papal throne from 43 to 67 A.D."[8] Reading this statement, I questioned how Peter could be the first pope in A.D. 43, since the church had been established in A.D. 33. I wondered why the church had allowed itself to exist without a head for 10 years This information contained deep inconsistency. I needed to examine more critically the dogma of the pope's primacy.

For years I had accepted without question the Catholic hierarchy's interpretation of Matthew 16:18 as the defense for Peter being the rock upon which the Catholic Church is built. Now I wanted to see what the Bible itself said. What, if anything, was conferred upon Peter by the words Jesus spoke? What privileges, if any, did Peter possess that the other apostles did not have? I reread the text contained in Matthew 16:16-19:

> Simon Peter answered and said, "You are the Christ, the Son of the living God." Jesus answered and said to him, "Blessed are you, Simon Bar-Jonah, for flesh and blood has not revealed this to you, but My Father who is in heaven. And I also say to you that you are Peter [petros], and on this rock [petra] I will build My church, and the gates of Hades shall not prevail against it. And I will give you the keys of the kingdom of heaven, and whatever you bind on earth will be bound in heaven, and whatever you loose on earth will be loosed in heaven."

I questioned myself about what Christ meant by the words "on this rock I will build My church?" According to the Catholic interpretation, Peter was the rock upon which Christ's church would be built. But if Christ wanted us to know that Peter was the foundation upon which His church would be built, would he not have been more explicit, saying something plainly like, "You are Peter, and upon you I will build my church"?

In Mark 8:29 and Luke 9:20, I read parallel passages to Matthew 16:18. Nothing is said about Peter as "the rock." In these verses, Jesus asks Peter "But who say you that I am?" and Peter replies: "You are the Christ" (Mark) or "The Christ of God" (Luke). In both of these passages, the matter under discussion is ended. If this doctrine was so important, why wasn't it addressed by both of these gospel writers?

In researching a Greek Lexicon for the word "rock," I discovered two words used for "Peter" and "rock" in Matthew 16:18. The Greek word for Peter is *petros* (the masculine gender). The word *petros* refers to a small detachment from a ledge, a stone, or a small pebble. The Greek word for rock is *petra* (the feminine gender) and refers to the ledge or cliff or a larger rock. I noted significant differences between these two words; they were not equivalent. What then is the rock, the *petra*, or the foundation upon which the church is built?

The Foundation of the Church

A noted Catholic theologian who read my first book, *A Change of Habit*, attempted to explain the concept of "Petrine Authority" in the following letter:

Dear Joanne,

For many centuries, Catholics have believed Jesus gave Peter a new name *Petros* meaning "rock." In the original Aramaic language, the word *Kepha* means "rock." Both of the "rocks" which Jesus referred to in the Aramaic are identical in meaning and there is no distinction in the gender, as there is in the Greek interpretation. Jesus' action in giving Simon the new name of "Peter" and then explaining what it means is highly significant in the context of biblical authority. He told Peter that He would receive the keys to the kingdom of heaven. "Keys" denote authority. Jesus then underlines the significance of this by explaining Peter's special authority in the kingdom of heaven by saying: "and whatsoever you bind on earth, shall be bound in heaven" (Matthew 16:19).

According to Bible scholars, the verse quoted in Matthew's text refers to the great truth expressed in the confession made by Peter when he said: "You are the Christ, the Son of the living God." As a child of God, Peter was but a small segment of the big cliff or rock upon which the church of Christ was built. Peter was not designated to be the cliff itself. In further research using my Bible concordance, I discovered that the word "rock" was used as a regular figurative expression in Old Testament scripture to express the all-powerful, supreme Jehovah:

And he [David] said: "The LORD is my rock and my fortress and my deliverer; The God of my strength, in whom I will trust" (2 Samuel 22:2-3).

For who is God, except the LORD? And who is a rock, except our God? (2 Samuel 22:32).

Many other examples in the New Testament refer to Jesus as the chief "cornerstone" or "solid rock" or the "firm foundation." In Matthew 21:42, Jesus explains to His adversaries that they must lay their foundation of faith and belief in Him:

Jesus said to them, "Have you never read in the Scriptures: 'The stone which the builders rejected Has become the chief cornerstone. This was the LORD'S doing, And it is marvelous in our eyes'?"

In this passage, Christ is called the foundation because through Him the Old and New Testaments become united. These words of Jesus are the proof that there is no other "rock" on which the church can place its confidence.

The Excuse of Authority

In Ephesians 2:19-22, the apostles and prophets are designated as the secondary foundation of the church and Jesus is depicted as the primary foundation, the chief cornerstone, the uniting force. Peter is given no special place in this description. All the other apostles occupy the same relationship as he does to the church; all are equally part of the secondary foundation:

Now, therefore, you are no longer strangers and foreigners, but fellow citizens with the saints and members of the household of God, having been built on the foundation of the apostles and prophets, Jesus Christ Himself being the chief cornerstone, in whom the whole building, being joined together, grows into a holy temple in the Lord, in whom you also are being built together for a dwelling place of God in the Spirit.

In reading further passages in Matthew 18, I noticed that shortly after Jesus said these words to Peter, the Savior bestowed upon the other apostles, the power of binding and loosing. He said:

> Moreover if your brother sins against you, go and tell him his fault between you and him alone. If he hears you, you have gained your brother. But if he will not hear, take with you one or two more, that "by the mouth of two or three witnesses every word may be established." And if he refuses to hear them, tell it to the church. But if he refuses even to hear the church, let him be to you like a heathen and a tax collector. Assuredly, I say to you, whatever you bind on earth will be bound in heaven, and whatever you loose on earth will be loosed in heaven (Matthew 18:15-18).

It became very apparent to me that the process of binding and loosing does not constitute any special privileges given to Peter alone. In John 20:21-23, Jesus again addressed his apostles:

> So Jesus said to them again, "Peace to you! As the Father has sent Me, I also send you." And when He had said this, He breathed on them, and said to them, "Receive the Holy Spirit. If you forgive the sins of any, they are forgiven them; if you retain the sins of any, they are retained."

My understanding of this passage deviates from the teaching I received as a Catholic. I was led to believe that this scripture confirmed the priest's authority to forgive sin. But Jesus had a different explanation when He made the above statement. When people reject Jesus' authority and teachings expressed through all the apostles (not just Peter), their sins are retained, or they are bound to their sins, but when they accept or obey the Gospel, their sins are forgiven, or they are loosed from their sins.

In a sense, all believers have the ability to declare that someone's sins are forgiven or retained based on whether or not they accept and obey the Gospel of Jesus. In 2 Timothy 2:2 we read: "And the things that you have heard from me among many witnesses, commit these to faithful men who will be able to teach others also."

I know that in the absolute sense only God can actually forgive or retain sins. However, the Gospel is God's power to save, and the act of preaching it makes it available to others. Those who bring the Gospel to others are not the ones making the decisions about whose sins to forgive and whose to retain, but they are able to assure the seeker of what is already true in heaven. Those who are not saved have the choice of either accepting or rejecting salvation. If individuals accept God's plan for their salvation, their sins are forgiven them. Should individuals reject this invitation, they are bound by their sins. So, too, the door of the kingdom is opened to all mankind, but when they reject entrance into the kingdom, the door is closed.

Not once, during this ministry, did Jesus give Peter extra privileges above the other apostles. In Matthew 18:1 we find the apostles asking Jesus this question: "Who then is greatest in the kingdom of Heaven?" Jesus answered their question with this response:

> Then Jesus called a little child to Him, set him in the midst of them, and said, "Assuredly, I say to you, unless you are converted and become as little children, you will by no means enter the kingdom of heaven. Therefore whoever humbles himself as this little child is the greatest in the kingdom of heaven" (Matthew 18:2-4).

Peter was a subject in the kingdom. In order for him to be acceptable before Jesus, he had to be humble, docile, and free from ambitious designs. If Jesus wanted us to know that Peter was to be His successor and the visible head of His church on this earth, He would have given him the honor as the greatest of His apostles.

The Origin of the Church

Throughout the American Catholic Churches today, I have encountered many Catholics who strongly disagree with the pope and those in the position of ecclesiastical authority within the church. One woman wrote the following:

Dear Joanne,

I was born and raised a Catholic during the pre-Vatican II era. Everything about my social and religious background has been influenced by my Catholic upbringing. I married young, and after 10 years, my husband left me for another woman — an ex-nun! When he left me, I left the Catholic Church and to this day I have not darkened the door of any church. I have tried to go back, but I'm confused and angry. I'm looking at the Catholic Church through a whole different set of eyes now. I'm involved in a neighborhood Bible study and I'm learning so many things I was not aware of as a Catholic. I have read your book and was amazed at how many scriptural references you have given to discredit many of the doctrines we learned and believed in catechism.

The one problem I have is understanding how so many people (even me) could have been duped into accepting the authority of the Pope. There are so many teachings I agreed to obey simply "on faith." Do you have any idea how the Catholic Church began and why they continue to remain a strong political force today?

Kim

Kim had asked an excellent question. While studying the history of the development of the New Testament church, I too, had wondered how such an institution as large as the Roman Catholic Church with its pope and hierarchy, could maintain its existence over hundreds of years without being questioned on its non-biblical doctrines. In answering Kim's question, my response was to begin an in-depth study and search of the scriptures. The church which Jesus founded had a beginning, and I needed to discover the time and place in God's Word.

About 600 years before Christ came into the world, Daniel foretold a kingdom which would never be destroyed, a kingdom that would be established during the days of the fourth earthly kingdom, the Roman kings, and it would break in pieces and consume all other kingdoms:

> And in the days of these kings the God of heaven will set up a kingdom which shall never be destroyed; and the kingdom shall not be left to other people; it shall break in pieces and consume all these kingdoms, and it shall stand forever (Daniel 2:44).

God, through the prophets, spoke of the time and place for the beginning of Christ's church. In Isaiah 2:2-3, God declared:

> Now it shall come to pass in the latter days That the mountain of the LORD'S house Shall be established on the top of the mountains, And shall be exalted above the hills; And all nations shall flow to it. Many people shall come and say, "Come, and let us go up to the mountain of the LORD, To the house of the God of Jacob; He will teach us His ways, And we shall walk in His paths." For out of Zion shall go forth the law, And the word of the LORD from Jerusalem.

From this prophetic declaration of God through Isaiah, I saw that God established three facts concerning the time and place of His church. First, the time for the beginning of the church would be in the last days. Second, God's house was to be exalted above all else, and all nations would flow into it. Third, the place where the church was to be established was in Jerusalem. In 1 Timothy 3:15 Paul explained that the house of God, to which the prophet referred, is the church of the living God:

[B]ut if I am delayed, I write so that you may know how you ought to conduct yourself in the house of God, which is the church of the living God, the pillar and ground of the truth.

Other prophetic scripture bears testimony to these facts:

Therefore thus says the LORD: "I am returning to Jerusalem with mercy; My house shall be built in it," says the LORD of hosts, "And a surveyor's line shall be stretched out over Jerusalem" (Zechariah 1:16).

Now it shall come to pass in the latter days That the mountain of the LORD'S house Shall be established on the top of the mountains, And shall be exalted above the hills; And peoples shall flow to it. Many nations shall come and say, "Come, and let us go up to the mountain of the LORD, To the house of the God of Jacob; He will teach us His ways, And we shall walk in His paths." For out of Zion the law shall go forth, And the word of the LORD from Jerusalem (Micah 4:1-2).

God's Word was beginning to reveal in detail, the time, the place, and the circumstances of the onset of the Lord's Church.

Matthew 3:1-2 tells that in the days of the Caesars and the Herods, John the Baptist, a cousin to Jesus, began preaching these words: "Repent, for the kingdom of heaven is at hand!"

According to Mark 1:15, when Jesus came, He declared the coming of His church with these words: "The time is fulfilled, and the kingdom of God is at hand." Having informed His disciples that He would build His church soon, Christ declared to the apostles in Matthew 16:28:

Assuredly, I say to you, there are some standing here who shall not taste death till they see the Son of Man coming in His kingdom.

Specific instructions were given the apostles concerning their waiting for the power of the Holy Spirit to descend upon them. This power was to accompany the establishment of the Lord's church. After Jesus had arisen from the dead and before His resurrection, He told His disciples:

Behold, I send the Promise of My Father upon you; but tarry in the city of Jerusalem until you are endued with power from on high (Luke 24:49).

The apostles were to wait at the designated place, the city of Jerusalem, where they would experience the outpouring of the Holy Spirit. Peter stood up with 11 other apostles and preached the message of repentance, baptism, and salvation to those who had crucified Jesus. The people hearing the gospel story were pricked in their hearts and cried out to Peter and the rest of the apostles, "What shall we do?" Peter replied:

Repent, and let every one of you be baptized in the name of Jesus Christ for the remission of sins; and you shall receive the gift of the Holy Spirit (Acts 2:38).

Thus, according to God's divine record, the first Pentecost following the resurrection of Jesus, marks the beginning of the church for which Jesus died. The kingdom of Christ was established between the time of Matthew 16:18 (when Jesus gave Peter the keys to the kingdom) and a few short months later at the time of Acts 2:47 in the year A.D. 33 in the city of Jerusalem. Having finished His earthly work, Jesus sat down at the right hand of God on the throne of David and was proclaimed the "king of kings and Lord of Lords (Acts 2:30-36).

The Growth of the Roman Catholic Church

During the early centuries after Christ, five great centers emerged — Jerusalem, Antioch, Alexandria, Constantinople, and Rome. Local churches, established after the time of Christ, had overseers or bishops. Those overseers were responsible local leaders who were on an equal basis authoritatively. However, smaller local churches had much respect for the opinions of the larger local churches and came to depend more and more on their counsel.

Rome was the largest city in the West during the early centuries, and the Christians associated much importance with the church there because of the significant events that had taken place in that city. Paul had suffered martyrdom there; the city had produced many outstanding Christian leaders; one of Paul's longest New Testament letters was written in Rome; and it was also in this city that the earliest persecution by the Roman State took place under the Emperor Nero in A.D. 64. So there were many reasons that influenced the smaller churches to look to the larger ones for guidance and leadership during the early years. Rome then, became the setting that permitted the claim for authority by the Christian leaders in Rome.

In A.D. 310, Christianity was declared the state religion by the Emperor Constantine. Multitudes of pagans were baptized into the Christian faith. Never truly converted, these pagans brought with them their own rituals and ceremonies. These traditions were eventually introduced into the Christian beliefs as doctrines of faith.

The Emperor Constantine retained the title "Pontifex Maximus," meaning High Priest of Christianity. Seeing that not all of his subjects were unified in their beliefs and practices, he called upon the Nicene Council to develop a creed of religious beliefs. Those who accepted the "Nicene Creed" became known as "Catholics." Those who continued to honor the Scriptures as their creed were Christians.

I recall my mother explaining how the Roman Catholic Church and the Eastern Orthodox Church were similar in many of their doctrines of faith. I often wondered why the Eastern Catholic Church had separated from the Western Catholic Church. The following information was helpful in my research:

> The Roman Church often had two Popes; and once there were three rival Popes at one time (The Great

West Schism 1378-1417). Even the famous Roman Catholic historian of the Popes, Pastor, admits that the Great Schism shook the authority of the church to its very foundation.[9]

About 60 years after the nominal Christianity was made the state religion the capital of the Roman Empire was moved from Rome to Constantinople. This soon led to a division of the empire into Eastern and Western and a corresponding division in the Catholic Church. Like many church divisions that have occurred since, it was more political than doctrinal. After the moving of the capital from Rome to Constantinople the Bishop of Rome was free to continue his usurpations without interference. He began to assume temporal power and appropriated the heathen designation of Pontifex Maximus. Roving hordes from the North began to overrun the Western Empire; the people began to look for leadership and the arrogant bishop stepped into the breach and before long began to be accepted as their leader. As aggressive as was the Bishop of Rome, it took several hundred years for him to reach the zenity of his power. The development was from the college of co-equal elders or bishops in every congregation to one bishop for each congregation. Then the diocesan bishop; after this five Patriarchs; still later, we have a period of rivalry between Rome and Constantinople; and then the period of the supremacy of Rome. During the fourth and fifth centuries the octopus of ecclesiasticism had developed to the stage of the five Patriarchs whose territory together comprised the known world. They were located at Jerusalem, Antioch, Alexandria, Constantinople and Rome. Rome, the old capital, and Constantinople, the new capital, had the advantage of the other claimants, and toward the close of the fifth century became rivals for the supremacy. As has already been stated, Rome had the opportunity to exercise self reliance because the Emperor was no longer near, and when the Western Empire was overthrown, in the year 451 A.D., practically all hinderances were removed. While Rome was practicing self reliance and entrenching herself as a political power, the Eastern Church was subservient to the political rulers. It is but natural that finally Rome should triumph. The final separation between Greek "Catholics "came about in the year 1054.[10]

Thus they became known as the "Greek Catholic Orthodox Church" and the Roman Catholic Orthodox Church. In the year A.D. 533, the ruler Justinian decreed that the bishop of Rome should be the head of the universal church

It seemed unbelievable to me that the entire Catholic Church's positions on papal authority, the proclamation of unscriptural doctrines, and the acceptance of tradition as teachings acceptable before God were politically motivated. I continued my historical research, hoping this was not the case.

As the church in Rome rose to her high pinnacle of power, it became known as the mother church. After the capital moved from Rome to Constantinople in the fourth century, the claim that Peter had been made Christ's vicar, that he was the first bishop of Rome and the popes of Rome were his successors, became forged and fabricated decrees of many councils. These decrees culminated in the famous "Isadorain Decretals" of the ninth century, which many scholars today acknowledge as forgeries.

The word "catholic" means "universal." The early Christians were part of the universal church, but they were not part of the Catholic Church as we know it today — with its popes, priests, other ecclesiastical authority, traditions, and liturgy. The present-day Roman Catholic Church evolved from the Roman religious leaders' desire to have authority over all other churches.

Jesus' Supreme Authority

In Matthew 28:18-20, our Lord confirmed His authority and power with these words:

> All authority has been given to Me in heaven and on earth. Go therefore and make disciples of all the nations, baptizing them in the name of the Father and of the Son and of the Holy Spirit, teaching them to observe all things that I have commanded you; and lo, I am with you always, even to the end of the age.

Jesus removed any doubts as to the position of power and authority in His church.

The amazing extent of the dominion of papal Rome throughout the ages fills me with wonder and sadness. I now see that the crux of the problem between the Roman Catholic Church and historic Christianity lies in the basis of authority. The Roman Catholic Church maintains that the basis for authority lies in the Roman Catholic Church. Historic Christianity maintains that final authority rests in the Scriptures, the revealed Word of God. Although the modern-day Roman Catholic Church believes the Bible to be authoritative, it does not believe the authority of the Bible is final; rather, the final word of authority is left to the pope and the traditions of the Roman Catholic Church.

Volumes have been written denying the pope as Peter's apostolic successor. My desire will always be to know what the Word of God says regarding matters pertaining to my soul. Paul must have known the confusion that would be caused because of various claims made by various churches. In writing to the church at Thessalonica he said:

> Let no one deceive you by any means; for that Day will not come unless the falling away comes first, and the man of sin is revealed, the son of perdition, who opposes and exalts himself above all that is called God or that is worshiped, so that he sits as God in the

temple of God, showing himself that he is God (2 Thessalonians 2:3-4).

The common denominator for all factions or doctrines is "unity in Christ." Christ is the center of God's platform for this unity:

[E]ndeavoring to keep the unity of the Spirit in the bond of peace. There is one body and one Spirit, just as you were called in one hope of your calling; one Lord, one faith, one baptism; one God and Father of all, who is above all, and through all, and in you all (Ephesians 4:3-6).

Whoever transgresses and does not abide in the doctrine of Christ does not have God. He who abides in the doctrine of Christ has both the Father and the Son (2 John 9).

New Testament Christianity — the faith of the early Christians — is God's call for all to be united with Him though His Son. Here is the answer to all religious authority. God calls not for another reformation but for a restoration of biblical teachings and a transformation into the likeness of His Son. Desirous to keep the unity of God's Spirit, I echo the pleadings of Isaiah:

For Zion's sake I will not hold My peace, And for Jerusalem's sake I will not rest, Until her righteousness goes forth as brightness, And her salvation as a lamp that burns. The Gentiles shall see your righteousness, And all kings your glory (Isaiah 62:1-2).

NOTE: A detailed summary of Roman Catholic practices and the approximate dates of their institution can be found on page 148.

Mary — The Most Misunderstood of All Women

👄〜

Among all the women who have ever lived, the mother of Jesus is the most celebrated, the most revered, the most portrayed, the most honored, and the most controversial figure in the world of religion. Volumes have been written praising her virginity, her motherhood, her virtues, and her position in heaven today.

I grew up praying to Mary, venerating her as the mother of God, and believing that every petition I requested of her would be granted. I was told by my mother, that as a newborn, I was covered with boils. After an application of "miraculous" water from the Shrine of Our Lady of Lourdes, the boils disappeared overnight. My devotion to Mary was always one of the deepest respect. I esteemed her as my heavenly mother and idolized her as I did my earthly mother. I wanted to model my life after this virtuous woman.

During my grade school years, I looked forward to participating in the yearly May procession that honored Mary's position as the "Mother of God" and "blessed among all women," who by her life "found favor with God" (Luke 1:28). As a culminating activity following the procession, a May

Queen and her court were selected to present bouquets of beautifully arranged flowers before a statute of Mary. Although I was never given that special honor, the ceremony led me to develop an intimate, prayerful relationship with Mary and I claimed her as the "Queen of My Heart!"

My Catholic instruction concerning the life and deeds of Mary depicted her as a tender, loving, compassionate woman. When the time came for God's final fulfillment of our redemption through Jesus Christ, Mary was the one chosen to become the "Mother of the Redeemer." It was Mary's seed (Jesus) who would bruise the heel of the serpent as prophesied in Genesis 3:15. It was Mary who would nurture Jesus at His birth, carry Him to safety in Egypt, guard Him in childhood, care for Him during His hidden years of youth, follow Him on His mission, stand beneath His cross, and await the coming of the Holy Spirit with His disciples after His death. I was taught that Mary had a closeness with Jesus unequal to that of any other human during His lifetime.

The issue of the mother of Jesus as "Queen of Heaven and all Angels," "Mediatrix of All Grace," and "Mother of the Church," while a major part of Catholic doctrine, is rejected by most non-Catholics. Most non-Catholics believe that exalting Mary beyond her divinely appointed role as the blessed earthly mother of Jesus, diminishes Christ's role as Redeemer and Lord. At Christmas, most non-Catholics tolerate Mary's limited appearances in greeting cards and manger scenes. But the rest of the year she is a victim of benign neglect. In bending over backwards to avoid excesses of veneration, the non-Catholic world has not always given the honor due this courageous and unpretentious woman of high character.

One of the most difficult adjustments I had to make upon becoming a New Testament Christian was to refrain from praying to Mary, while speaking to her son, Jesus. A great part of my devotional life had been spent invoking her help. Even now I can recall reciting the litanies exalting her many titles, praying the "Hail Mary" in adoration of her name and position, and wondering about the many apparitions that have caused thousands to proclaim her divine healing powers.

In my early days as a New Testament Christian, I asked questions such as, "What is the proper balance of reserve and respect for Mary? What would God want me to believe and how would God want me to honor the woman He chose to become the earthly mother of His divine Son, Jesus?"

Mary in the Bible

I have discovered these answers within God's Word and have examined the historical data that led to Mary's receiving an honor not given to any other earthly being. I have also prayed for wisdom and guidance in sharing this information with so many of my friends who have been led astray in the crossfire of a centuries old debate between Protestants and Catholics.

I first read about Mary in the gospel records of Matthew 1:18-25 and Luke 1:26-38; 2:1-7. The gospels tell about Mary's betrothal to Joseph of Nazareth. Before their marriage, Mary was with child by the Holy Spirit. Luke 1:26-49 records the visit of the Angel Gabriel to Mary with these words:

> Now in the sixth month the angel Gabriel was sent by God to a city of Galilee named Nazareth, to a virgin betrothed to a man whose name was Joseph, of the house of David. The virgin's name was Mary. And having come in, the angel said to her, "Rejoice, highly favored one, the Lord is with you; blessed are you among women!" But when she saw him, she was troubled at his saying, and considered what manner of greeting this was. Then the angel said to her, "Do not be afraid, Mary, for you have found favor with God. And behold, you will conceive in your womb and bring forth a Son, and shall call His name JESUS. He will be great, and will be called the Son of the Highest; and the Lord God will give Him the throne of His

father David. And He will reign over the house of Jacob forever, and of His kingdom there will be no end." Then Mary said to the angel, "How can this be, since I do not know a man?" And the angel answered and said to her, "The Holy Spirit will come upon you, and the power of the Highest will overshadow you; therefore, also, that Holy One who is to be born will be called the Son of God. Now indeed, Elizabeth your relative has also conceived a son in her old age; and this is now the sixth month for her who was called barren. For with God nothing will be impossible." Then Mary said, "Behold the maidservant of the Lord! Let it be to me according to your word." And the angel departed from her. Now Mary arose in those days and went into the hill country with haste, to a city of Judah, and entered the house of Zacharias and greeted Elizabeth. And it happened, when Elizabeth heard the greeting of Mary, that the babe leaped in her womb; and Elizabeth was filled with the Holy Spirit. Then she spoke out with a loud voice and said, "Blessed are you among women, and blessed is the fruit of your womb! But why is this granted to me, that the mother of my Lord should come to me? For indeed, as soon as the voice of your greeting sounded in my ears, the babe leaped in my womb for joy. Blessed is she who believed, for there will be a fulfillment of those things which were told her from the Lord." And Mary said: "My soul magnifies the Lord, And my spirit has rejoiced in God my Savior. For He has regarded the lowly state of His maidservant; For behold, henceforth all generations will call me blessed. For He who is mighty has done great things for me, And holy is His name."

In a Greek Lexicon, I discovered two Greek words for the word "blessed." The root word for Elizabeth's greeting in Luke 1:42 is *eulogeo*. When Elizabeth told Mary she was "blessed among women," as had Gabriel, Mary understood that she was specially favored or well-spoken of by God. This Jewish blessing could not be revoked or reversed. These words would have lived and throbbed in Mary's mind as a perpetual sign of God's affirmation and approval. Being "blessed" meant that God favored and trusted her enough to burden her with one of the most difficult roles of a lifetime. She knew that her son was God enfleshed in a man's body, yet during His earthly life He would be considered a failure and ultimately crucified!

The other Greek word for "blessed" used by Mary's cousin is *makaria*. This term relates to being "satisfied, fulfilled, full of God." The context in which Elizabeth spoke this prophetic word was significant. Mary was to be full of God because she believed that what the Lord had said to her would be accomplished. Mary didn't close herself off from God, but with trust in her heart she set forth to execute His will.

After Mary returned from visiting her cousin Elizabeth, the Word of God tells us that Joseph took Mary as his wife. The gospels then record that Mary gave birth to Jesus Christ, the only begotten Son of God and the Savior of the world. The story about Jesus' birth is recorded in Matthew 2:1-15 and Luke 2:7-18. We learn how the shepherds received the birth announcement, how the angels affirmed Jesus' uniqueness, and about the wealthy Gentile astrologers later bringing exotic gifts and worshiping at the feet of this Jewish child. Scripture says, "But Mary kept all these things and pondered them in her heart" (Luke 2:19).

God's Word tells of Mary and Joseph's long journey southward from Nazareth to Bethlehem, their flight to Egypt to protect Jesus from the murderous campaign of Herod, and then their return to Nazareth where Jesus spent the remainder of His boyhood days.

Mary is mentioned only four more times in the gospels. Her next appearance is recorded at the wedding feast in Cana recorded in John 2:1-12. Here, Mary witnesses the first miracle of her son Jesus as He turns water into wine:

On the third day there was a wedding in Cana of Galilee, and the mother of Jesus was there. Now both Jesus and His disciples were invited to the wedding. And when they ran out of wine, the mother of Jesus said to Him, "They have no wine." Jesus said to her, "Woman, what does your concern have to do with Me? My hour has not yet come." His mother said to the servants, "Whatever He says to you, do it." Now there were set there six waterpots of stone, according to the manner of purification of the Jews, containing twenty or thirty gallons apiece. Jesus said to them, "Fill the waterpots with water." And they filled them up to the brim. And He said to them, "Draw some out now, and take it to the master of the feast." And they took it. When the master of the feast had tasted the water that was made wine, and did not know where it came from (but the servants who had drawn the water knew), the master of the feast called the bridegroom. And he said to him, "Every man at the beginning sets out the good wine, and when the guests have well drunk, then the inferior. You have kept the good wine until now!" This beginning of signs Jesus did in Cana of Galilee, and manifested His glory; and His disciples believed in Him. After this He went down to Capernaum, He, His mother, His brothers, and His disciples; and they did not stay there many days.

As a Catholic, I was taught to believe that Jesus listened to his mother whenever she presented Him with a request and honored her petitions. My intercessions to Mary never ceased, for I believed she could identify with every one of my needs. My mother had an intense devotion to Mary. I would hear her pray to her in time of crisis and felt as confident as she that her requests would be granted. I was not aware that Mary's role at the wedding in Cana did not support her position as an intercessor before God. I did not know that Jesus alone had the power of intercession:

And whatever you ask in My name, that I will do, that the Father may be glorified in the Son. If you ask anything in My name, I will do it (John 14:13-14).

For there is one God and one Mediator between God and men, the Man Christ Jesus (1 Timothy 2:5).

I could not find any scripture that verified the Catholic Church's position on Mary's sharing mediating efforts with Jesus in Heaven. Yet, the Vatican Council II reaffirmed the doctrine of Mary's mediation in these teachings:

The motherhood of Mary, in the order of grace, continues uninterruptedly from the consent which she loyally gave at the Annunciation and which she sustained without wavering beneath the cross, until the eternal fulfillment of all the elect. Taken up to heaven, she did not lay aside this saving office but by her manifold intercession continues to bring us the gifts of eternal salvation. By her maternal charity she continues to care for the brethren of her Son, who still journey on earth surrounded by dangers and difficulties until they are led into their blessed home. Therefore the Blessed Virgin is invoked in the Church under the titles of Advocate, Helper, Benefactress, and Mediatrix. This, however, is so understood that it neither takes away anything or adds anything to the dignity and efficacy of Christ the one Mediator.[11]

It is so plainly clear to me that this doctrine is in violation of the major theme of the New Testament, that Jesus Christ is the only path to reconciliation with God. Throughout Hebrews we read about Jesus as the payment for sin, now assuming His place as High Priest and Advocate at the right hand of God (Hebrews 8:1; 9:24; 10:10-18).

On the basis of His complete identification with mankind and His full participation in the human experience, Scripture tells of Jesus sympathizing with my plight and continually making intercession for me (Hebrews 2:16-18; 4:14-15; 7:25). I obtain confident access to my God through Jesus, and there is no need for any other mediator. "Nor is there salvation in any other, for there is no other name under heaven given among men by which we must be saved" (Acts 4:12).

The next scene where Mary is mentioned in the gospels occurs at Capernaum. She and the Lord's brothers wanted to speak to Jesus. He was very busy preaching to the multitudes. He answered this request by teaching that spiritual ties are far more important, binding, and sacred than fleshly ties. Jesus respected His mother, but He did not deify her. It seems as if He implied a gentle rebuke of her interference with His work as Savior of mankind:

> Then His mother and brothers came to Him, and could not approach Him because of the crowd. And it was told Him by some, who said, "Your mother and Your brothers are standing outside, desiring to see You." But He answered and said to them, "My mother and My brothers are these who hear the word of God and do it" (Luke 8:19-21; also recorded in Mark 3:31-35).

In reading this scripture more carefully, I observed that Jesus responded to the crowd gathered in front of Him rather than to the individual who had delivered his mother's request. He made it clear that "My mother and My brothers are these who hear the word of God and do it." Jesus left no doubt that obedience to God's will is the spiritual test of being His disciple. This relationship outranks earthly ties which are temporal while spiritual ties are eternal. He calls those who do His Father's will by the endearing names of "brother and sister and mother."

In John 19:25-27, I read one of the most tender scenes in the sacred writings of the gospel story. Mary, the earthly mother of Jesus, is standing at the foot of the cross witnessing the tragic scene of her son's crucifixion. During His last hours on earth, Jesus asks John, one of His disciples, to take care of His mother after His death. Even while dying, Jesus taught from the cross the importance of the commandment which says, "Honor your father and mother."

Now there stood by the cross of Jesus His mother, and His mother's sister, Mary the wife of Clopas, and Mary Magdalene. When Jesus therefore saw His mother, and the disciple whom He loved standing by, He said to His mother, "Woman, behold your son!" Then He said to the disciple, "Behold your mother!" And from that hour that disciple took her to his own home.

Mary was always exalted as my "individual mother" and "Mother of the Church" during the years I believed and taught Roman Catholic doctrine. In his encyclical "Magnae Dei Matris," Pope Leo XIII described Mary's position in these words:

> By the very fact that she was chosen to be the Mother of Christ, Our Lord, Who is at the same time our brother, she was singularly endowed above all other mothers with the mission of manifesting and pouring out her mercy upon us. Moreover, if we are indebted to Christ in that he has shared with us in some way the right, peculiarly His own, of calling God our Father and possessing him as such, to Christ's loving generosity we are similarly indebted for sharing in His right to call Mary Mother and to possess her as such. Just as the most holy Virgin is the Mother (*Genetrix*) of Jesus Christ, so she is the Mother of all Christians, whom indeed she bore (*generavit*) on Mt. Calvary amid the supreme throes of the Redeemer; also, Jesus Christ is as the first-born of all Christians, who by adoption and Redemption are his brothers.[12]

The honor and respect I have for Mary today is based upon God's Word, the only secure anchor I have for truth and spiritual knowledge. This passage in scripture explains that the relationship Mary had with Jesus, as His earthly mother, was now to exist between His beloved disciple John and His mother, following His death on the cross. No other disciple was given this privilege. I found it difficult to rationalize how this commandment (that was given only to John) could be used to further validate the position of Mary as our heavenly mother today.

Acts 1:14 is the last recorded appearance of Mary in the scriptures. The gospel writer Luke describes Mary in prayer with the apostles in the upper room in Jerusalem during the interval between our Lord's ascension into heaven and the arrival of the Holy Spirit at Pentecost.

> These all continued with one accord in prayer and supplication, with the women and Mary the mother of Jesus, and with His brothers.

The idea of Jesus having natural brothers was a teaching that was completely foreign to me as a Catholic. I could not comprehend God's allowing another child to enter Mary's womb after the birth of Jesus. Although marriage was seen as an honorable institution within the Church, childbearing rather than sexual pleasure in marriage was taught and encouraged. Mary's virginity was emulated as the most praiseworthy of all of Mary's virtues. I upheld the teaching that Mary remained a perpetual virgin during her lifetime and encouraged many young girls to follow her example.

The scriptural teaching in Matthew 13:54-56 gave me reason to change my belief in Mary's perpetual virginity. In reading this passage, I learned that Mary was the mother of other children and the doctrine of perpetual virginity is contrary to the teachings revealed to us by God's Holy Spirit.

> And when He had come to His own country, He taught them in their synagogue, so that they were astonished and said, "Where did this Man get this wisdom and these mighty works? Is this not the carpenter's son? Is not His mother called Mary? And His brothers James, Joses, Simon, and Judas? And His sisters, are they not all with us? Where then did this Man get all these things?"

The context of this scripture leaves no doubt in my mind that James, Joseph, Simon, and Judas were literal brothers of Jesus and children of Mary and Joseph. The scriptures are silent regarding the time, place, and circumstance of Mary's death. God chose not to have this made known to future generations.

Mary — What Happened?

Throughout this study, I have asked myself this question: "What occurred through the centuries of time that allowed the mother of Jesus to become a victim of unscriptural myths and false veneration?"

Charles Russell states that the worship of the Virgin Mary was introduced to meet and gratify and to attach itself upon, the superstition which had long prevailed amongst the heathen in respect to Isis, Diana, and other pagan goddesses, who had millions of worshippers.[13]

When the Emperor Constantine declared Christianity a national religion, many of the converts brought with them their pagan idolatries, especially their worship of the pagan goddesses Isis and Diana. To satisfy the superstitious minds of these former heathens, Mary was introduced as a powerful intercessor who could equal and even surpass the supposed powers of these goddesses. To further satisfy these converts, statutes of the Blessed Virgin were made before which they could kneel and pray for her intercession just as they did before their pagan goddesses.

Ralph Woodrow, in his book *Babylon Mystery Religion*, presents a history of various goddesses whose statues of mother and child were worshiped by different cultures. He also states that "in the pagan religions, the mother was worshiped as much (or more) than her son" (p.21). The church at Ephesus encouraged worship to Mary calling her the "Mother of God" (*theotokos* is the term used for "Mother of God" meaning godbearer). The Council of Ephesus decreed that Mary should be worshiped, making it an official doctrine in A.D. 431. Woodrow states further:

It was in this city that Diana had been worshiped as the goddess of virginity and motherhood from primitive times. She was said to represent the generative powers of nature and so was pictured with many breasts. A tower-shaped crown, a symbol of the tower of Babel, adorned her head.

When beliefs are held by a people for centuries, they are not easily forsaken. So church leaders at Ephesus — as the falling away came — also reasoned that if people would be allowed to hold their ideas about a mother goddess, if this could be mixed into Christianity and the name of Mary substituted, they could gain more converts. But this was not God's method. When Paul had come to Ephesus in earlier days, no compromise was made with paganism. People were *truly* converted and destroyed their idols of the goddess (Acts 19:24-27). How tragic that the church at Ephesus in later centuries compromised and adopted a form of mother goddess worship, the Council of Ephesus finally making it an official doctrine![14]

With the passing of the centuries, adoration and veneration of Mary grew and gradually became crystallized by the Roman Catholic Church into a system of dogmas under the term of "Mariology."

Mary in Catholic Doctrine

The Roman Catholic Church has never ceased to glorify Mary as the "Mother of God," "Queen of Heaven," and "Mediatrix" in its pronouncements over the centuries. In supporting the Church's belief in its veneration of Mary, the following declarations have been made by various leaders over a period of time:

Pope Pius IX
God has committed to Mary the treasury of all good things, in order that everyone may know that through

her are obtained every hope, every grace, and all salvation. For this is his will, that we obtain every thing through Mary.

Pope Leo XIII
As no man goes to the father but by the son, so no one goes to Christ except through his mother.

Cardinal Alphonsus de Liguori
Mary is called "the gate of heaven because no one can enter that blessed kingdom without passing through her."

Pope Pius XII
It is the will of God that we should have nothing which is not passed through the hands of Mary.[15]

Second Vatican Council
By her maternal love, Mary cares for the brethren of her son who still journey on earth. Therefore, the Blessed Virgin is invoked by the church and the titles of Advocate, Auxiliatrix, Adjutrix and Mediatrix. These, however, are to be so understood that they neither take away nor add anything to the dignity and efficacy of Christ, the one mediator. For no creature could ever be classed with the incarnate Word and Redeemer.[16]

There is no question that in the annals of Christianity, Mary will always stand out as a woman of character. It is tragic, however, that the veneration and worship of Mary encouraged by those in ecclesiastical authority have led many sincere God-fearing Catholics astray in accepting mythology regarding Mary. Please don't misunderstand this statement. I will always uphold Mary as a honorable role-model for every member of Christ's church. Her unswerving faith held firm despite the extraordinary demands she encountered during her life with Jesus. On the other hand, I can not encourage anyone else to honor unscriptural teachings, traditions, and myths that have not been authenticated in God's holy Word.

The Bible and Catholic Doctrine

There is no evidence from teachings that were divinely inspired and revealed by God's Holy Spirit that the following doctrines proclaimed by the Roman Catholic Church are acceptable before God.

The Doctrine of the Immaculate Conception

This doctrine, made official in 1854, teaches that Mary was preserved from sin at the moment of her conception. This was to be God's perfect act of purification to prepare Mary to bear the Son of God in her womb. This doctrine was rejected for a period of 1,200 years before Pope Pius IX defined this as an official doctrine of the Roman Catholic Church in 1854. Four years later, an apparition of Mary in Lourdes, France, greeted a young peasant girl, Bernadette Soubirous with this statement: "I am the Immaculate Conception."

Romans 3:23 states, "for all have sinned and fall short of the glory of God." In 1 John 1:8 we read: "If we say that we have no sin, we deceive ourselves, and the truth is not in us." Each and every human who has ever lived to the age of choosing is guilty of sin in the sight of God, with the only exception being Jesus (Hebrews 4:15; 1 Peter 2:22).

Mary herself states, "My soul magnifies the Lord, And my spirit has rejoiced in God my Savior" (Luke 1:46-47). Mary recognized her own need for redemption. Also, if Mary was not worthy to be the mother of Jesus because of her sinful nature, then the same can be said about her mother, grandmother, and so on.

In 1 Kings 8:46 we read: "[T]here is no one who does not sin." Ecclesiastes 7:20 states: "For there is not a just man on earth who does good And does not sin."

The text of Genesis 3:15 does not prove the Immaculate Conception of Mary. God speaks to the serpent who has beguiled Eve saying, "And I will put enmity Between you and the woman, And between your seed and her Seed; He shall bruise your head, And you shall bruise His heel." The

Hebrew text reads "He" or "It" not "She" (meaning Mary) shall bruise. This is confirmed in Romans 16:20 where Paul says, "And the God of peace will crush Satan under your feet shortly." This is God's first promise and prophecy of Christ in God's Word.

In conclusion, I now firmly believe that the doctrine of the Immaculate Conception is in complete opposition to the teachings in God's Word.

The Doctrine of Mary's Perpetual Virginity

The Catholic Church teaches as a doctrine of faith that Mary was a virgin before Christ's birth (which scripture explicitly states) and remained a virgin throughout her lifetime. This doctrine was endorsed by the Council of Trent in 1545.

In Matthew 1:24-25 we read this statement, "Then Joseph, being aroused from sleep, did as the angel of the Lord commanded him and took to him his wife, and did not know her till she had brought forth her firstborn Son."

In the Old Testament in Exodus 13:2, we read of the Lord's command to Moses, "Consecrate to Me all the firstborn, whatever opens the womb among the children of Israel, both of man and beast; it is Mine." Marriage as an honorable institution was authorized by God. Mary did not defile or desecrate the marital bond she had with Joseph but maintained her love and devotion to him through a physical union with him. Jewish law required that the husband and wife were obligated to render to one another their conjugal rights. Paul reaffirmed this in his letter to the Church at Corinth when he said:

> Let the husband render to his wife the affection due her, and likewise also the wife to her husband. The wife does not have authority over her own body, but the husband does. And likewise the husband does not have authority over his own body, but the wife does. Do not deprive one another except with consent for a time, that you may give yourselves to fasting and prayer; and come together again so that Satan does

not tempt you because of your lack of self-control (1 Corinthians 7:3-5)

Doctrine of Mary's Bodily Assumption into Heaven

The bodily assumption of Mary into the realms of heaven was honored by Pope Gregory I in A.D. 543. In 1950, Pope Pius XII proclaimed Mary's Assumption an official doctrine of the Roman Catholic Church. He declared and defined it to be a divinely revealed dogma that the Immaculate Mother of God, the ever Virgin Mary, having completed the course of her earthly life, was assumed body and soul into heavenly glory.[17]

One of the curses brought upon mankind by Adam and Eve's disobedience to God in the Garden of Paradise was that death would consume their earthly bodies. God said, "In the sweat of your face you shall eat bread Till you return to the ground, For out of it you were taken; For dust you are, And to dust you shall return" (Genesis 3:19).

A clear, concise statement of the Word of God in Romans 5:12 says this about death, "Therefore, just as through one man sin entered the world, and death through sin, and thus death spread to all men, because all [have] sinned."

In Hebrews 9:27, the writer says that death will come to all of mankind: "And as it is appointed for men to die once, but after this the judgement."

The tremendous words in Psalm 90, speaks of the brevity of human life:

> For we have been consumed by Your anger, And by Your wrath we are terrified. You have set our iniquities before You, Our secret sins in the light of Your countenance. For all our days have passed away in Your wrath; We finish our years like a sigh (Psalm 90:7-9).

From the scriptures already considered, I believe there are definite, inescapable conclusions that must be recognized regarding the subject of death and Mary's bodily assumption into heaven:

1. Adam's deliberate disobedience to God assured death for all humans, including Mary, the mother of Jesus.

2. Death is the cessation of life in the physical realm, the separation of the soul from the body and the consequent decay of the body.

3. The Bible reveals the bodily assumption of Jesus into heaven. Only two other bodily ascensions are mentioned: Enoch (Hebrews 11:5) and Elijah (2 Kings 2:11).

Relying on God's Word, my view of death and my future destiny must always be rooted in a reverent acceptance of Scripture. John 12:48 states that in my personal judgment before God, I will be judged on my knowledge of God's Word and my obedience to His commands. The Roman Catholic Church has invented theories and assumptions, but God speaks with definiteness and gives us all the information He wants us to know in this life.

I never realized the importance of the above papal decrees upon the Catholic psyche until I did an in-depth study of the history of their evolution. Like a domino effect, one dogma affected the other until all dogmas were unquestionable and acceptable to the Catholic mind — including my own! However, honest study of the Bible has the same effect in reverse — the truth sets free.

When Jesus was presented at the temple in Jerusalem as an infant, a man named Simeon blessed Him:

> Then Simeon blessed them, and said to Mary His mother, "Behold, this Child is destined for the fall and rising of many in Israel, and for a sign which will be spoken against (yes, a sword will pierce through your own soul also), that the thoughts of many hearts may be revealed" (Luke 2:34-35).

With his soul's eyes, Simeon saw the link between Christ's rejection and Mary's own heartache, and from then on the sword of these prophetic words pierced and penetrated with each event in her life. I believe today that if Mary knew the prayers, adoration, and veneration she is receiving instead of her Son her wounds of sorrow would be deepened. Various devotions, such as the Rosary, litanies, novenas, pilgrimages, and even apparitions that have occurred in her name would astonish her and cause her tremendous sadness.

Because of her exemplary life, Mary is a shining model for all Christian's hope and can be a unifying example for both Catholics and non-Catholics in this context. However all must recognize and accept that Jesus alone is the "Mediator," "Savior," "Intercessor," and "Redeemer" for all mankind. Jesus is the one who opens his arms to those who are despondent, guilt-ridden, and hopeless and says, "Come to Me, all you who labor and are heavy laden, and I will give you rest" (Matthew 11:28).

Once I devoted myself to the study of God's Word, the scales of tradition that blurred my sight fell away. I then began to see God's glory, to know His wisdom, and to feel the refreshment and assurance this knowledge brings.

I shared the teachings from God's Word with my dear mother. She could see how much obedience to the Scriptures had changed my life. My mother has always been a deeply religious woman with a receptive heart. From childhood, she had been taught in the Russian Orthodox faith to form a strong religious bond with the Virgin Mary. This bond increased in strength when she became a Roman Catholic upon her marriage to my father. Consequently, her loyalty to Mary took on an urgency that overshadowed the need she felt for baptism.

One day she said to me, "Joanne, I know I need to be baptized, but I can't give up Mary! She has helped the entire family in our times of deepest needs." Her devotion to Mary had become so intense, that it superseded her devotion to Jesus' command to put Him on in baptism.

We continued to study the Bible together out of devotion to God. Our souls were riveted to understanding the powerful messages of God's Word. Finally, God helped my mother realize that she was wrong to pray to or through Mary rather than her Son. Before making her final confession before the congregation of believers, she wrote these words:

My deep faith in God and Jesus compelled me to be properly baptized. Because I was a Roman Catholic, it was a difficult decision for me. I always called upon Mary, the mother of Jesus, to help me in raising my children. The decision was: either to continue viewing Mary as my intercessor, or to be baptized into Christ. For several years I longed to be baptized. I have read the Bible many times, but my love for Mary was so great. Although, Joanne kept reminding me, it was Jesus who heard my requests. When I heard, "Do you realize you are insulting Mary by going to her instead of her Son?" — that finally did it.[18]

Mary, a young Nazarene handmaiden chosen by God to bear His Son, is a role model for all Christians who desire to excel in humility and submissiveness. To understand her role as the mother of Jesus is to understand her place in God's plan for life. The Bible is silent regarding Mary's perpetual virginity, freedom from personal sins, and bodily assumption into heaven.

I believe that if Mary were to return to earth today, her plea to all believers in her Son would be the same request she made to the servants at the wedding feast in Cana, "Whatever He [Jesus] says to you, do it" (John 2:5).

The Bible emphasizes Jesus as possessing the preeminence in all things and being all sufficient in leading men and women to God:

And He is the head of the body, the church, who is the beginning, the firstborn from the dead, that in all things He may have the preeminence. For it pleased the Father that in Him all the fullness should dwell, and by Him to reconcile all things to Himself, by Him, whether things on earth or things in heaven, having made peace through the blood of His cross ... For in Him dwells all the fullness of the Godhead bodily; and you are complete in Him, who is the head of all principality and power (Colossians 1:18-20; 2:9-10).

Eternal Truths and Catholic Doctrine

Catholics today are leaving the Church by the millions. I have known many who are products of Catholic schools, religious education programs, religious rituals, and liturgy, who after years of being a Roman Catholic have walked away from a heritage that provided emotional security, traditions, and orthodox beliefs. What has precipitated this departure?

I believe there are two answers. One viewpoint is that today's society has come to observe religion simply as personal and subjective, echoing the exaltation of the individual above all else, even above one's responsibilities to God and to others. With each person supreme in his or her own right, the question arises, "Who needs God?"

Another answer to this problem can be found in the words of Jesus, "And you shall know the truth, and the truth shall make you free" (John 8:32).

The history of man reveals a continuing search for truth in the realm of religion. The poet John Greenleaf Whittier wrote:

We search the world for truth; we cull
The good, the pure, the beautiful,
From graven stone and written scroll,

And all old flower-fields of the soul;
And, weary seekers of the best,
We come back laden from the quest,
To find that all the sages said
Is in the Book our mothers read.[19]

Neither you nor I can find truth by ourselves. Why is this? God's Word proclaims that it is only by divine revelation in the Bible that we can learn what is truth and how to be saved:

O LORD, I know the way of man is not in himself; It is not in man who walks to direct his own steps (Jeremiah 10:23).

There is a way that seems right to a man, But its end is the way of death (Proverbs 16:25).

He who trusts in his own heart is a fool, But whoever walks wisely will be delivered (Proverbs 28:26).

One of the letters I received from a reader of my first book addressed these issues of truth, doctrine and community:

Dear Joanne,

My entire life (of 35 years) has been spent in searching for God. When I was 16 years old, I thought about entering a convent, but then I was involved in dating, and decided I would like to get married instead. I went to college and limited my involvement with God to attending Sunday Mass. Eventually, I excluded God altogether from my life. Even though I was not a practicing Catholic, I had a deep hunger for a close relationship with God. Once I was invited to a Bible study on campus. I saw where there could be joy and zeal in religion. I began to frequent these studies. I remember when Bible reading and prayers brought a movement to my soul. I began hearing that the teachings in the Catholic Church were unscriptural and full of man-made traditions that distorted God's truths. I left the Catholic Church, believing I could find God in another religion. It wasn't long before I discovered I had joined a cult. I remained in this religious group for six years. Throughout this period of time, I searched constantly for an inner peace that seemed attainable, but to no avail.

I now have five children and want to bring them up in the ways of the Lord. My husband is non-religious and does not care about their religious training. I need to find a church that is strongly grounded in the Scriptures and offers personal involvement with a warm loving outreach to non-believers. Since I have become involved in my own personal Bible study, I am able to find biblical proof of many of the doctrinal errors that are preached on TV. I am interested in the New Testament Church you describe in your book, *A Change of Habit*. Perhaps you can recommend one I can visit in the area where I live. I look forward to hearing from you soon.

Sandy

In reading Sandy's letter, I could feel the spiritual hunger crying out from her soul. She had developed a deep personal relationship with God through His Word. Her faith in Him was a vital part of her life. Now she needed to experience and share this knowledge and faith in a community of believers. I was able to direct her to a New Testament congregation where the Bible was taught, respected, and practiced.

Faith is one of the most important issues in my relationship with God. In Hebrews 11:6 we read, "But without faith it is impossible to please Him, for he who comes to God must believe that He is, and that He is a rewarder of those who diligently seek Him."

Growing up Catholic, my faith rested on external manifestations of prayers and devotions developed by those in the magesterium (teaching authority) of the Church. Praying before statues, participating in rituals, partaking of the sacraments, and expressing my emotions through the liturgy meant identifying with God in these special ways.

My faith was never developed through reading, understanding, and applying the Word of God to my life. Romans 10:17 showed me how God accepted my faith in Him: "So then faith comes by hearing, and hearing by the word of God." I have come to have faith in Scripture as the living and dynamic Word of God. His Word nourishes my soul with spiritual food, sustains, comforts, and encourages me in times of doubt and shows me those truths to be honored in this life and in eternity. I understand how the Psalmist felt when he wrote these inspiring words: "Your word is a lamp to my feet And a light to my path" (Psalm 119:105).

I have titled this chapter "Eternal Truths and Catholic Doctrine" because of the discovery I made of the wide chasm that exists between the teachings of Christ and the apostles and the teachings in Roman Catholicism.

A Look at the Original Church

If you and I could be miraculously transported in time back to the days of early Christianity, we would be surprised to discover a church unlike the traditional churches we know today. Modern-day churches have incorporated many doctrines and traditions that are not authenticated in any of the teachings given to the New Testament church by Jesus.

The meaning of the word "church" is translated from the Koine Greek word *ecclesia* which means "a called out group of people." This *ecclesia* is used to refer to all of God's people in the new covenant period, not just the church in Jerusalem, the first congregation established on that first Pentecost after Christ's resurrection. Other congregations then began to be planted in various parts of the Roman Empire. Paul wrote to "the church of God which is at Corinth" (1 Corinthians 1:2). The church in Philippi was referred to as "the saints in Christ Jesus who are in Philippi"

(Philippians 1:1). The saints in Thessalonica were referred to as "the church of the Thessalonians in God the Father and the Lord Jesus Christ" (1 Thessalonians 1:1). And so, the word "church" was used to refer to a number of congregations of God's people established in a particular locality.

In Colossians 1:18, the church is referred to as a body with Jesus Christ as its head:

> And He is the head of the body, the church, who is the beginning, the firstborn from the dead, that in all things He may have the preeminence.

Christ being the head, all the body is subject to Him. Every individual member is under His authority. Christ is not visibly present on this earth, but His spirit is present "in the midst" of His disciples wherever two or three gather together in His name (Matthew 18:20).

When Jesus was about to leave this earth to ascend to His Father in Heaven, He charged His apostles to "wait for the Promise of the Father" and told them to "tarry in the city of Jerusalem until you are endued [clothed] with power from on high" (Acts 1:4; Luke 24:49). The apostles were the first leaders, chosen by Christ for His Church. God says in Hebrews 2:3-4:

> [H]ow shall we escape if we neglect so great a salvation, which at the first began to be spoken by the Lord, and was confirmed to us by those who heard Him, God also bearing witness both with signs and wonders, with various miracles, and gifts of the Holy Spirit, according to His own will?

These apostles have no successors (no other human being can be an apostle) and the apostles have "once and for all" given the doctrine of Jesus Christ to the world. No new doctrines were to be established after Christ's death, nor traditions enacted. In 2 Timothy 3:16-17, the Word of God is emphatic that Scripture alone is to reveal God's perfect will for you and me:

> All Scripture is given by inspiration of God, and is profitable for doctrine, for reproof, for correction, for instruction in righteousness, that the man of God may be complete, thoroughly equipped for every good work.

There is no scriptural evidence the apostles required some hierarchical, inter-congregational organization in the local church. We do know that Paul left Titus on the island of Crete to organize the believers and local church bodies and "set in order the things that are lacking, and appoint elders in every city" (Titus 1:5). These elders were to become overseers of each congregation and direct its affairs. These men were also referred to as "bishops, presbyters, pastors, and shepherds" of God's flock. In Acts 14:23 God's plan called for a plurality of elders in every congregation. God clearly states the qualifications necessary to ordain a member of the congregation an elder:

> This is a faithful saying: If a man desires the position of a bishop, he desires a good work. A bishop then must be blameless, the husband of one wife, temperate, sober-minded, of good behavior, hospitable, able to teach; not given to wine, not violent, not greedy for money, but gentle, not quarrelsome, not covetous; one who rules his own house well, having his children in submission with all reverence (for if a man does not know how to rule his own house, how will he take care of the church of God?); not a novice, lest being puffed up with pride he fall into the same condemnation as the devil. Moreover he must have a good testimony among those who are outside, lest he fall into reproach and the snare of the devil (1 Timothy 3:1-7).

> For a bishop must be blameless, as a steward of God, not self-willed, not quick-tempered, not given to wine, not violent, not greedy for money, but hospitable, a lover of what is good, sober-minded, just, holy, self-controlled, holding fast the faithful word as he has been taught,

that he may be able, by sound doctrine, both to exhort and convict those who contradict (Titus 1:7-9).

The New Testament church also included in its leadership, a group of men called "deacons." These men were not bishops or overseers, but were chosen to be servants to the church. These were men upon whom the elders could always depend in accomplishing any specific work. We read about their first being appointed in Acts 6:1-8 and about their qualifications in 1 Timothy 3:8-13.

Nowhere in the New Testament is there an example of one official overseeing one or more congregations. Neither is there an example of a body of officials exercising any kind of oversight over more than one congregation. In the New Testament congregation, an evangelist labored under the direction of the elders of that congregation. His obligation was to teach and preach the Gospel, both to the saved and to the lost. The members were called "saints," and each was given a talent for the welfare and edification of the church (Ephesians 4:11-12).

All the members of the New Testament church believed in Jesus. They put their faith and trust in Him alone and not in some statement of doctrine about Him. Because of their strong belief in Christ, they contended for His teaching and had no other creed. In Acts 2:42 the Bible tells us that the first church continued steadfastly in the apostles' doctrine.

If you or I were to visit a group of believers in the early church, we would likely find them assembled to listen to the words of Jesus as spoken by the apostles. We would observe them praying, singing, keeping the Lord's Supper, and contributing of their means.

There would be no mention of a human creed spoken among this group of Christians. I remember learning the "Apostles Creed" in catechism classes. I can recite it today from memory. While it says much that is true, it is not a creed that was written or required by the apostles.

The New Testament church was very simple. There were no synods, councils, conventions, associations, or conferences of delegates from different congregations constituting an ecclesiastic legislative body. There were only local congregations of believers taught and shepherded by local elders. There was no higher authority except for Jesus. All the elders were equal. Even Peter considered himself a fellow elder. Each congregation was autonomous. Any other ecclesiastical body that is not organized as Christ had established exists without His authority.

In contrast with the simplicity of the New Testament church government, I know how highly organized the Roman Catholic system of government has become. In my study of church history I have always been intrigued with the way the Roman Catholic Church developed its highly sophisticated form of hierarchy over the centuries. Today, the pope at Rome has become a worldwide spiritual leader, who claims to be the direct successor of Peter, asserting that Peter was the head of the early church. Below him is a sacred college composed of cardinals, 12 patriarchs, more than 600 archbishops and bishops, and many monsignors and priests. Through these magesterium the Roman Catholic Church is governed.

I have had the opportunity to attend a Jewish synagogue and have seen a similarity in their form of worship with the worship service of the Roman Catholic Church. Many of its ceremonies stem from the Jewish culture. There is a reason for this. After the legalization of the Christian Church in A.D. 345, the lords, Roman senators, or any other persons of high rank were given the title of priest. These priests began to substitute their ideas and their cultural observances into doctrinal beliefs. As part of the respect that was accorded them, these priests were permitted to wear distinctive clothing and to have candles and emblems carried before them. Because the serfs and peasants could not read, they were unfamiliar with biblical doctrine; therefore the lords (now priests) became the highest ranking authority in the church. They assumed that this important position qualified them to become mediators between God and others.

Over a period of 400 years, from the Council of Trent to the second Vatican Council, many abuses in teachings, creeds, ceremonies, and rituals departed from the sound doctrine of the Scriptures. Paul foresaw this happening and warned Christ's flock with these words:

> Let no one deceive you by any means; for that Day will not come unless the falling away comes first, and the man of sin is revealed, the son of perdition, who opposes and exalts himself above all that is called God or that is worshiped, so that he sits as God in the temple of God, showing himself that he is God (2 Thessalonians 2:3-4).

> Now the Spirit expressly says that in latter times some will depart from the faith, giving heed to deceiving spirits and doctrines of demons (1 Timothy 4:1).

The death of Jesus marked the end of the Mosaic dispensation and the beginning of the Christian era. This marked the fulfillment of the covenant with Israel as a nation and the offer of salvation to the Gentiles upon the same terms offered to the Jews and the replacement of the Old Law with the perfect law of Christ (Matthew 5:17; Galatians 2:15-16; 3:19-29; Hebrew 8:18-19).

How well I remember being able to recite the Ten Commandments. Each time I went to confession, I was taught to examine my conscience according to my obedience or disobedience to each of these laws of the old covenant. There were times when I couldn't remember my sins, so in order to receive the blessings from the sacrament of confession, I would make up sins hoping to obtain absolution from the priest. I did not yet realize that while Jesus wanted me to keep the commandments, He was the one who could cover me with His blood and make me pure in God's sight if I was only obedient to Him.

The Catholic Sacraments

I learned, honored, obeyed, and taught Roman Catholic doctrines believing they were the embodiment of God's manifold wisdom. I was unfamiliar with the scriptures used to defend these doctrines. Hence, I approached every article of faith with statements from one of the Councils or with definitions I had learned in the Baltimore Catechism.

The doctrines of the Mass, supremacy of the pope, tradition and scripture, and Mary have been given consideration in previous chapters. In the remainder of this chapter, I would like to address specific doctrines taught in Roman Catholicism and compare them with the teachings of Jesus and His apostles.

Doctrine of the Sacraments and Grace

Roman Catholicism teaches that the sacraments are visible channels through which the grace of God comes to each individual as they participate in these sacraments. The word *sacramentum* is synonymous with the Greek word *mysterion*. There are seven sacraments originating in ancient traditions and adopted as official Roman Catholic and Greek Orthodox doctrine in the 13th century.

As a very young child I learned the names of the seven sacraments: baptism, confirmation, holy orders, Eucharist, penance, matrimony, and anointing of the sick. I was told these sacraments were given to the church by Christ. It was deeply impressed upon my mind that these sacraments were to nourish, strengthen, develop personal sanctification, and serve as the avenue by which I expressed my faith in Christ and gave worship to God.

The Catholic Church uses a wide range of sacramentals in the administration of these sacraments. Holy water, ashes, relics, bells, candles, incense, medals, crucifixes, statues, and specific gestures are used as visible signs of God's blessings. I remember identifying them as the "bells and smells" of Catholic worship.

Besides using rites and ceremonies in the presentation of these sacraments, I was taught that a special grace was conferred upon me when I partook of any of these sacraments. These graces were called sanctifying grace and sacramental grace. Sacramental grace helped me carry out the particular purpose of a given sacrament. Sanctifying grace was a special grace that gave my soul a new life in God.

I have been unable to find anywhere in Scripture, the portioning of God's grace into various categories. I have discovered in Ephesians 2:8-9 the way God says I can partake of His grace:

> For by grace you have been saved through faith, and that not of yourselves; it is the gift of God, not of works, lest anyone should boast.

Grace is the love and mercy of God in action. God showed me His mercy in love when He sent His Son to bear my sins in His own body on the cross at Calvary. God's grace comes as His free gift. I cannot buy it or earn it. The grace of God is unconditional and saves the soul. I am not saved by the sacraments or any other work, but by the grace of God through Christ Jesus. This doesn't mean that I can continue in sinning, but that I am freed from the penalty of the law in order to do God's will (Romans 6-8). Paul calls grace God's indescribable gift (2 Corinthians 9:15). All I can do is accept God's grace through obedience to Jesus.

God told Paul and us that, "My grace is sufficient for you, for My strength is made perfect in weakness" (2 Corinthians 12:9). God says that His grace will teach people how to live:

> For the grace of God that brings salvation has appeared to all men, teaching us that, denying ungodliness and worldly lusts, we should live soberly, righteously, and godly in the present age (Titus 2:11-12).

The concept of sacraments is not taught in the Bible either. Had God wanted me to know about the doctrine of the sacrament, He would have declared it to be a mystery. A mystery was a spiritual truth which could not be explained except by divine revelation. But after it was explained by a man chosen by God, it was no longer a mystery. In Mark 4:11 Jesus tells His apostles: "To you it has been given to know the mystery of the kingdom of God." In Ephesians 1:9 and 3:8-12 we are told that God has revealed the mystery to all.

Upon completing his letter to the Christians at Rome, Paul concludes with these words:

> Now to Him who is able to establish you according to my gospel and the preaching of Jesus Christ, according to the revelation of the mystery kept secret since the world began but now has been made manifest, and by the prophetic Scriptures has been made known to all nations, according to the commandment of the everlasting God, for obedience to the faith — to God, alone wise, be glory through Jesus Christ forever. Amen (Romans 16:25-27).

What a wonderful proclamation Paul made. God chose him to deliver the doctrines of His heavenly message and to write them in all of his epistles for His church. Paul reaffirms this in his letter to the Ephesians when he says:

> [A]nd for me, that utterance may be given to me, that I may open my mouth boldly to make known the mystery of the gospel (Ephesians 6:19).

Through this message, God is able to put His stamp upon my thinking, feeling, and living. I don't need to participate in man-made sacraments that have become traditionalized in the Catholic Church for this to occur. His grace is shown in the transformation of my actions because of God's grace working in me.

Doctrine of Baptism

Several months after I left the convent, I had the opportunity to visit with a relative whom I had not seen in years. Both she and her husband were atheists and had raised their daughter to be a non-believer in God. One evening, as I baby-sat this precious five-year-old, I remembered my Catholic teaching on baptism. The old Baltimore Catechism stated that baptism is a sacrament that gives our souls the new life of sanctifying grace by which we become children of God and heirs of heaven. I was always taught that it was important to baptize infants shortly after their birth since infants who die with original sin on their souls would not see heaven. I was taught that these children would live in a place of natural happiness called Limbo. I looked at this sweet, innocent child and believed she belonged with God in heaven. I wanted her to be accepted before God. I knew what I must do.

After telling her about God, who He was, and how much He loved her, I then told her about Jesus and how He had died a terrible death so that she and I could be with Him in heaven. I spoke to her about being baptized and explained to her how important this action was to God. I then told her that God would make her soul shine like a beautiful diamond, once the ugly stain of original sin was removed from her soul. I explained the meaning of grace (a special gift God would place in her heart) and reassured her that once she was baptized God would come into her heart and make her His very own child. I can still see the look of wonder and expectation in her innocent eyes as she agreed to let me perform the rite of baptism.

Walking over to the sink, I sprinkled a few drops of water on her forehead saying, "I baptize you in the name of the Father, and of the Son, and of the Holy Ghost. Amen." At the moment this occurred, I truly believed this child would go straight to heaven. I promised to be her godparent throughout her life, seeing that she would be guided in the teachings of the Roman Catholic faith. This promise was never fulfilled in the Catholic faith, but I continue to pray for her daily that she will come to the knowledge of what she must do to be saved and obey the Gospel before it is too late.

Of all the sacraments Catholicism has claimed were taught by Jesus, baptism is the only one He set forth as a commandment. In Matthew 28:19-20 Jesus sent the apostles into all the world to make disciples and to baptize in the name of the Father, Son, and Holy Spirit those who had been taught:

Go therefore and make disciples of all the nations, baptizing them in the name of the Father and of the Son and of the Holy Spirit, teaching them to observe all things that I have commanded you; and lo, I am with you always, even to the end of the age.

Mark's record of the Great Commission says:

And He said to them, "Go into all the world and preach the gospel to every creature. He who believes and is baptized will be saved; but he who does not believe will be condemned" (Mark 16:15-16).

In Acts 2, tells us that 3,000 were baptized for the remission of their sins:

Now when they heard this, they were cut to the heart, and said to Peter and the rest of the apostles, "Men and brethren, what shall we do?" Then Peter said to them, "Repent, and let every one of you be baptized in the name of Jesus Christ for the remission of sins; and you shall receive the gift of the Holy Spirit. For the promise is to you and to your children, and to all who are afar off, as many as the Lord our God will call." And with many other words he testified and exhorted them, saying, "Be saved from this perverse generation." Then those who gladly received his word were baptized; and that day about three thousand souls were added to them (Acts 2:37-41).

Paul's statement in Romans 6:3-4 adds to our understanding:

Or do you not know that as many of us as were baptized into Christ Jesus were baptized into His death? Therefore we were buried with Him through baptism into death, that just as Christ was raised from the dead by the glory of the Father, even so we also should walk in newness of life.

I will never forget the concern and frustration I experienced when I was confronted with my own baptism in a Bible study. I believed I had been saved as an infant. I was taught that the stain of original sin was washed away the moment the water was sprinkled over my infant head. Yet, in the New Testament the only valid candidates for baptism were those who had been taught, believed, repented, and confessed Jesus as Lord. They were then immersed in water. As an infant, I was unable to fulfill any of these requirements. In Acts 8:12, I read:

But when they believed Philip as he preached the things concerning the kingdom of God and the name of Jesus Christ, both men and women were baptized.

None of the 10 examples of conversion in Acts (which contains the historic development of the church) record a single instance or word about the baptism of infants. In further study of God's Word, I began to realize I didn't need to be baptized as an infant to meet heaven's approval because I was not born with the guilt of sin. In 1 John 3:4 I read where sin is the transgression of God's law: "Everyone who sins breaks the law; in fact, sin is lawlessness" (NIV).

I read how sin occurred in my life once I reached the age of accountability:

But each one is tempted when he is drawn away by his own desires and enticed. Then, when desire has conceived, it gives birth to sin; and sin, when it is fullgrown, brings forth death (James 1:14-15).

I asked myself, "How could I transgress the laws of God I knew nothing about as an infant?" If children were sinners,

Jesus would never have held them up as examples of purity and humility:

> Assuredly, I say to you, unless you are converted and become as little children, you will by no means enter the kingdom of heaven (Matthew 18:3).

> Let the little children come to Me, and do not forbid them; for of such is the kingdom of heaven (Matthew 19:14).

> Assuredly, I say to you, whoever does not receive the kingdom of God as a little child will by no means enter it (Mark 10:15).

None of the above passages gave me any evidence that Jesus considered children guilty of sin and in need of salvation. Even in the Old Testament which Jesus quoted often, I read these words:

> You were perfect in your ways from the day you were created, Till iniquity was found in you (Ezekiel 28:15).

> Truly, this only I have found: That God made man upright, But they have sought out many schemes (Ecclesiastes 7:29).

> The son shall not bear the guilt of the father, nor the father bear the guilt of the son (Ezekiel 18:20).

These passages were indisputable truth that from my birth, until the age when I was old enough to know the difference between right and wrong, I was safe in the arms of Jesus!

I realized the sins of Adam and Eve were far-reaching, and being human, I too, had transgressed God's laws over and over. I was born into a world filled with influences that led me away from the purity God demands of those who desire to come before His presence.

Baptism was no longer an option for me, but a command from Jesus Himself. The Bible teaches that once I reached the age of accountability, I needed to be baptized in order to be saved. Since I had not done so, even though I believed I was a good person, I would remain lost for all eternity.

I believed I was saved long before I was baptized until I read the passage in Mark where Jesus placed baptism before salvation, "He who believes and is baptized will be saved" (Mark 16:16). Paul taught that I had to be baptized to put on Christ: "For as many of you as were baptized into Christ have put on Christ" (Galatians 3:27).

Before my mother's baptism at the age of 78, she posed this question to me: "What about the thief on the cross and all those individuals who could not accept the terms of pardon Christ desired. Will they be lost as well?"

I explained to her that those individuals lived and died before Christ's death and that they would be judged according to the laws of their dispensation. The thief on the cross in Luke 23:39-43 died under the Mosaic dispensation. This penitent thief had confessed his sins, reproved his companion, defended Jesus, and then asked Jesus to remember him in His kingdom. This action gained this thief Paradise, a place where I want to be in eternity.

My faith and trust in Jesus prompted me to obey my Lord's command and become scripturally baptized. Immersed in water for the remission of my sins, I was washed in the blood of Christ. This act brought me a new spiritual identity, changed my relationship and status with God, and established a confident hope for my eternal destiny. I now belong to a "royal priesthood" (1 Peter 2:9) and I wear the robes of righteousness, knowing that God's Holy Spirit will direct my life until the day God calls me home. The great salvation that was purchased for me by One who loved me so deeply is now mine, with all the blessings I have been promised in His Word.

Doctrine of Confirmation

One of the most exciting times of my life was my confirmation at the age of 12. This sacrament is considered a rite of passage into adulthood. I became a member of the

Catholic Church at my infant baptism, but when I was confirmed, I took upon myself all the responsibilities of a Catholic adult. I remember having to study apologetics for weeks, knowing that I would be questioned on my ability to defend my Catholic faith before anyone who inquired.

Confirmation was considered such a special event that the bishop of the local diocese presided over the ceremony. Through this sacrament and the "laying on of hands" by the bishop, I would be empowered by God's Holy Spirit to proclaim the teachings of the Catholic Church throughout my life. During the ceremony I would renew those promises that were made for me at my baptism by my godparents. I remember the bishop giving each of us who were being confirmed a tap on the cheek. While some giggled, I remember accepting this event very seriously as this tap was to remind me that I was to suffer anything, even death, for my faith.

Shortly after becoming a Christian, I began a study about the Holy Spirit. I was confused as to how the Spirit of God operated in my life. I believed that my body was the temple of the Holy Spirit as I had been taught this doctrine as a child, but I no longer believed that God's Holy Spirit dwelt within me as a result of my confirmation. I now needed to learn what the Scriptures taught regarding the indwelling of the Spirit of God.

In my study of God's Word, I learned the Holy Spirit is God. In Acts 5:3-4 I read:

> But Peter said, "Ananias, why has Satan filled your heart to lie to the Holy Spirit and keep back part of the price of the land for yourself? While it remained, was it not your own? And after it was sold, was it not in your own control? Why have you conceived this thing in your heart? You have not lied to men but to God."

Since the Holy Spirit is part of the Godhead, He is eternal, all-knowing, all-powerful, and ever-present. If He is a personality, then the Holy Spirit can hear, speak, command, become grieved, and be insulted. In view of who the Holy

Spirit is, I was puzzled as to His presence within me. Upon my baptism into Christ, Peter promised in Acts 2:38 that I would receive the "gift of the Holy Spirit." In the course of my study, I came upon a passage in Matthew 18:20 where Jesus promised to be in every assembly where two or three are gathered in His name. In reading various other passages of scripture, I came to realize that the personhood of Jesus is in heaven, sitting at the right hand of God (Acts 7:56), but where and whenever we serve the Lord, we come before His divine presence.

During the early days of the church, the Holy Spirit came to the apostles on Pentecost (Acts 2:1-4), at Samaria (Acts 8:14-18), at the household of Cornelius (Acts 10:44), at Ephesus (Acts 19:6), and at Corinth (1 Corinthians 12:4-11) through miraculous endowments and operations. This is one way the Spirit of God was in the apostles at the same time (John 14:17) and in the prophets (1 Peter 1:10-11). The Holy Spirit, personally, was not in the man, but rather the Spirit's presence was there through the miraculous gifts. The Spirit of God was present representatively.

Today, the Spirit is in me by the influence of His teaching through His Word. I now understand that it was the Spirit of God who enlightened and converted me through His Word. Before Jesus died, He told His apostles that He would send the Comforter (or His Holy Spirit) who would guide them into all truth. I realize now that the Spirit operates through the Word of God and independent of this Word we could never know whether there is any Holy Spirit. Consequently, all the teaching on the sacrament of confirmation is unscriptural. Apart from the inspiration of the apostles and prophets, it is impossible for the Holy Spirit to communicate His message.

Doctrine of Penance

The magesterium of the Roman Catholic Church teaches that Jesus gave His authority to His apostles to forgive sins. This authority was passed down through chain of command to those in the priesthood today. They use these scriptures to defend their position:

> And I also say to you that you are Peter, and on this rock I will build My church, and the gates of Hades shall not prevail against it. And I will give you the keys of the kingdom of heaven, and whatever you bind on earth will be bound in heaven, and whatever you loose on earth will be loosed in heaven (Matthew 16:18-19).

> And when He had said this, He breathed on them, and said to them, "Receive the Holy Spirit. If you forgive the sins of any, they are forgiven them; if you retain the sins of any, they are retained" (John 20:22-23).

Catholics believe the Holy Spirit became the source of authority for priests after their ordination to the priesthood to forgive sin in God's name. When they said the words, "I absolve you of your sins, in the name of the Father, and of the Son, and of the Holy Spirit," this was a sign that sins were forgiven before God. When I was growing up this sacrament was known as the sacrament of penance. Today it is known as the sacrament of reconciliation.

Penance is the sacrament by which the sins I committed after my baptism are forgiven through the absolution of the priest. I remember going into the confessional, kneeling before a screened window covered by a dark curtain, and saying, "Bless me Father, for I have sinned. It has been five days (or whatever time had elapsed) since my last confession." I would then confess those sins I could remember over that specific period of time. Depending on the seriousness of my sins, the priest would give me a penance (prayers to say or certain acts to perform) before he would then grant me absolution.

God knew the frailty of our sinful nature and our inclination to sin. He knew also that a remedy was necessary for those of us who needed reconciliation. He did not intend that we go through a human mediator, but instead He encouraged us to come directly to the throne of forgiveness. In His tender love and mercy, God promised to forgive us if we come to Him through Jesus. In 1 John 1:9 we read, "If we confess our sins, He is faithful and just to forgive us our sins and to cleanse us from all unrighteousness."

Each time I sin, God demands my repentance, not an act of penance as if I could earn forgiveness. God spoke through the prophet Isaiah, telling us to turn away from those sins that continually enter our thoughts and actions:

> Let the wicked forsake his way, And the unrighteous man his thoughts; Let him return to the LORD, And He will have mercy on him; And to our God, For He will abundantly pardon (Isaiah 55:7).

God alone has the power to forgive sin. In John 20:21-23, Jesus tells His disciples that He is sending them out into the world. This can be considered as John's account of the Great Commission. Their power to remit or retain sin was through their preaching of the gospel message as revealed to them through the Holy Spirit. Those who heard and obeyed the message could be assured that their sins were forgiven; those who rejected the message were condemned. There is no biblical evidence that God gave the apostles or anyone the power to forgive sin other than through proclaiming His message of forgiveness through Jesus.

The aforementioned doctrines are the essential core theology of Roman Catholicism. These doctrines must be received on faith by all Catholics. Failure to accept these beliefs would be considered a mortal sin. Dying in this state would bring on eternal punishment.

Loyalty to Truth

Although the Catholic Church accepts the Bible as its final authority, it rejects the biblical teaching of salvation by grace through faith in Christ and total obedience to His Word. The Catholic Church holds to and honors traditions they claim are commandments of the Lord, endorsed by the apostles or their successors. It claims that these commandments and practices have been handed down by word of mouth from one generation to another with these teachings confirmed in the New Testament.

No one can prove that any unwritten commandment or practice was ever taught or given authorization by Jesus or the inspired apostles. In fact, 2 Timothy 3:16-17 tells us that God gave written Scripture to equip us completely for every good work.

God does not want men to mingle their man-made doctrines with His commandments. Jesus rebuked the scribes and Pharisees for this very thing:

> Hypocrites! Well did Isaiah prophesy about you, saying: "These people draw near to Me with their mouth, And honor Me with their lips, But their heart is far from Me. And in vain they worship Me, Teaching as doctrines the commandments of men" (Matthew 15:7-9).

God warns against altering His Word:

> For I testify to everyone who hears the words of the prophecy of this book: If anyone adds to these things, God will add to him the plagues that are written in this book; and if anyone takes away from the words of the book of this prophecy, God shall take away his part from the Book of Life, from the holy city, and from the things which are written in this book (Revelation 22:18-19).

We should all search for and embrace the truth. Jesus said:

> But the hour is coming, and now is, when the true worshippers will worship the Father in spirit and truth; for the Father is seeking such to worship Him.God is Spirit, and those who worship Him must worship in spirit and truth (John 4:23-24).

Jesus also said, "I am the way, the truth, and the life. No one comes to the Father except through Me" (John 14:6).

Inasmuch as Jesus declared himself to be truth, we may safely conclude that to love truth is to love Jesus.

As each of us delves into a study of the truths Jesus spoke, the mind of God will be revealed to us and He will make clear His will for our lives. We will discover the Bible to be a complete and perfect guide for directing our hearts and lives.

Each of us must be willing to respect the truth of Jesus' teachings as recorded in Scripture. We must keep our worship and service to Him uncorrupted by the commandments, practices and innovations introduced without God's authority. The obligation to find and accept spiritual truth is on you and me, regardless of the cost we must pay. Truth is opposed only by the forces of darkness, evil and fear. Anyone or anything that tries to keep you from seeking truth in the Bible is not of God.

Holding to truth can exact a high price. The truth cost Jesus His life. So too with the early Christian martyrs who refused to worship Caesar rather than God and Christ. It deprived Paul of his standing in the religious community and caused him to suffer many hardships (2 Corinthians 11:24-27). But what a small price to pay for the privilege of being able to live as God's child and to one day dwell in His house.

How wonderful the assurance of Jesus' words to those who search, believe, obey, and live by His truth:

If you abide in My word, you are My disciples indeed. And you shall know the truth and the truth shall make you free (John 8:31-32).

But seek first the kingdom of God and His righteousness, and all these things shall be added to you (Matthew 6:33).

Ask, and it will be given to you; seek, and you will find; knock, and it will be opened to you. For everyone who asks receives, and he who seeks finds, and to him who knocks it will be opened (Matthew 7:7-8).

The Royal Priesthood

Nothing excites me more today than to know that I am a member of God's royal priesthood. God describes my position as His priest in these words:

> [Y]ou also, as living stones, are being built up a spiritual house, a holy priesthood, to offer up spiritual sacrifices acceptable to God through Jesus Christ ... But you are a chosen generation, a royal priesthood, a holy nation, His own special people, that you may proclaim the praises of Him who called you out of darkness into His marvelous light; who once were not a people but are now the people of God, who had not obtained mercy but now have obtained mercy (1 Peter 2:5, 9-10).

These marvelous words are almost incomprehensible to grasp as I reflect on who I was and who I am becoming today. Once dead in sin, I am now alive because of the deep love and forgiveness shown me by a merciful God. In reverential awe and gratitude, I bow in worship before Him as His priest. God confirmed my priesthood through the song of the 24 elders in Revelation 5:9-10:

And they sang a new song, saying: "You are worthy to take the scroll, And to open its seals; For You were slain, And have redeemed us to God by Your blood Out of every tribe and tongue and people and nation, And have made us kings and priests to our God; And we shall reign on the earth."

As a former nun, never in my most vivid dream could I have ever imagined myself as a priest in God's service. Many of my fellow Catholics envisioned themselves wearing a white collar and a long flowing cassock, embroidered in red. But today, without these special adornments, I can claim this title with God's blessings.

The honor and position of being one of God's royal priests required that I accept the terms of the priesthood of the new covenant I made with Christ as my Mediator.

Long ago, God made a promise to Abraham:

Now the LORD had said to Abram: "Get out of your country, From your family And from your father's house, To a land that I will show you. I will make you a great nation; I will bless you And make your name great; And you shall be a blessing. I will bless those who bless you, And I will curse him who curses you; And in you all the families of the earth shall be blessed" (Genesis 12:1-3).

The first element of this promise was a pledge to Abraham that he would have a numerous family (both physical and spiritual). The second element was that God would be God to both families, and the third was that each of these families would become heirs of an everlasting inheritance. Finally, God said that the world would be blessed because of their existence. Another agreement God made with Abraham was the covenant of circumcision which served to distinguish the Hebrew race from all others. God pledged a promised inheritance upon fulfillment of this covenant.

Several hundred years after God made His covenant with Abraham, He entered into a covenant relationship with the people of Israel through the giving of the Law of Moses (Deuteronomy 5:1-5). This covenant contained laws and ordinances relating to the different kinds of sacrifices and established the Levitical priesthood.

Under the old covenant there were genealogical, marital, and physical qualifications for the priest. God stipulated that His priests were to possess certain requirements outlined in Leviticus 21, including:

1. The priest had to come from the tribe of Levi.

2. He could not join himself to a divorcee or to an immoral woman.

3. Physically, he was to be without blemish; he could not be bald, nor have any cuttings in his flesh. He could not be blind, nor deformed in any part of his body.

The priest in the old covenant was the only one permitted to enter the tabernacle to make atonement for the people. The function of the priest was to be the mediator between God and the people. A special day was set aside (the Day of Atonement) whereby sacrifices were offered by the priest for the sins of the people. The Jewish people looked upon the old covenant as the power of God for the salvation of the seed of Abraham according to the flesh.

Obviously, the priesthood under the Levitical laws was literal and very limited. There were some individuals who presumed to serve as priests, but they could not trace their descent to the right source. When the examination of the genealogical records confirmed this, they were thrust from their office (Ezra 2:62).

God's covenant with the people of Israel lasted until Christ came "born of a woman, born under the law, to redeem those who were under the law" (Galatians 4:4-5).

In Hebrews 7:11-12 the writer declares that God has made a change in the priesthood:

Therefore, if perfection were through the Levitical priesthood (for under it the people received the law), what further need was there that another priest should rise according to the order of Melchizedek, and not be called according to the order of Aaron? For the priesthood being changed, of necessity there is also a change of the law.

The old covenant was characterized by a kingdom with physical priests; whereas the new covenant provided for a kingdom of spiritual priests with Christ as the sole mediator before God. Hebrews 8 expresses this beautifully:

Now this is the main point of the things we are saying: We have such a High Priest, who is seated at the right hand of the throne of the Majesty in the heavens, a Minister of the sanctuary and of the true tabernacle which the Lord erected, and not man. For every high priest is appointed to offer both gifts and sacrifices. Therefore it is necessary that this One also have something to offer. For if He were on earth, He would not be a priest, since there are priests who offer the gifts according to the law; who serve the copy and shadow of the heavenly things, as Moses was divinely instructed when he was about to make the tabernacle. For He said, "See that you make all things according to the pattern shown you on the mountain." But now He has obtained a more excellent ministry, inasmuch as He is also Mediator of a better covenant, which was established on better promises. For if that first covenant had been faultless, then no place would have been sought for a second. Because finding fault with them, He says: "Behold, the days are coming, says the LORD, when I will make a new covenant with the house of Israel and with the house of Judah — not according to the covenant that I made with their fathers in the day when I took them by the hand to lead them out of the land of Egypt; because they did not continue in My covenant, and I disregarded them, says the LORD. For this is the covenant that I will make with the house of Israel after those days, says the LORD: I will put My laws in their mind and write them on their hearts; and I will be their God, and they shall be My people. None of them shall teach his neighbor, and none his brother, saying, 'Know the LORD,' for all shall know Me, from the least of them to the greatest of them. For I will be merciful to their unrighteousness, and their sins and their lawless deeds I will remember no more." In that He says, "A new covenant," He has made the first obsolete. Now what is becoming obsolete and growing old is ready to vanish away.

Of all the doctrine and theology I was taught as a nun, I was never introduced to the concept of a covenant let alone ways in which I could become a servant (or minister) in this type of agreement. I was not encouraged to read the Bible, interpret its message, and apply its truths to my life. Not until I began to search for truth within the pages of God's Word and discover His plan for my life was I completely aware of my status before God.

One of the few scriptures I remember learning throughout my years as a Roman Catholic was read during the ceremony of my investiture as a nun. These words from Matthew left an indelible impression upon my mind and led me to the religious life I now practice today:

> Then Jesus said to His disciples, "If anyone desires to come after Me, let him deny himself, and take up his cross, and follow Me" (Matthew 16:24).

Throughout my life as a Roman Catholic and especially during my years as a nun, I longed to carry my cross like Jesus and serve Him in the greatest way possible. I would write lengthy letters to Him during the required periods of meditation. I would like to share with you an excerpt from one of these meditations:

Dearest Jesus,

As I ponder Your love for me, I think of the many sacrifices You have made for all of mankind. You came to earth to accept the lowly life of a human being and live with creatures far beneath Your status as God. You became a brother to us as You walked among the rich and famous and the poor and lowly making Yourself one of us. You were always being subject to the will of men unequal to Your Godliness until at last they nailed You to a cross — far beneath the royalty You should have received as God. Your whole life was one of a continual refusing of Yourself as You helped to carry others' burdens and share their sorrows.

Help me to emulate Your lifestyle, Jesus. Let me draw from the depth of Your well of humility and patience. Walk with me each step of my life so that I can hear You say to me one day in the realms of Your heavenly kingdom, "Well done, my good and faithful servant."

Forgive me, Lord, for those sins that keep creeping into my life and grant me the grace to obey Your commandments. Lead me in Your ways, dear Jesus, as I do love You and I want to serve You always.

I believe to this day that this prayer was heard before the throne of God. I also believe that God knew my heart and provided many opportunities to occur in my life in order that I could accept the terms of His new covenant and become His priestly servant.

Under the terms of this new covenant, God promised to put His laws into my mind and the mind of all who choose to serve Him (Hebrews 8:10). As a Catholic, I learned to memorize and apply the Ten Commandments given to Moses on Mt. Sinai and other laws required by the Catholic Church. I treasured those commandments as a letter from God, inscribed on two tablets of stone. I was not aware of the life-giving power God had implanted in His Word, but God enlightened my understanding by means of His inspired Word and inscribed His words upon my heart through prayer and study. One of the many passages in His Word that affected me deeply explains, "Whoever commits sin also commits lawlessness, and sin is lawlessness" (1 John 3:4).

I had never grasped the true hideousness of sin and the need to become totally pure in God's presence until I began to study God's Word. I knew in my heart I had committed sins, uttered statements I should not have made, and left undone duties I should have done. Responding to those teachings I had been trained to believe as a Catholic, I was convinced that if I made a fervent act of contrition in the confessional before a priest God would save me from the guilt and penalty of my sins. Many times, after leaving the confessional, I was never persuaded in my mind I had been completely forgiven although I had received absolution from the priest. I would then hasten to perform many acts of penance to reassure myself that God would honor my works. However, upon reading Acts 16:31, I felt Gods' assurance when Paul said, "Believe on the Lord Jesus Christ, and you will be saved, you and your household."

My heart was touched by this truth contained in God's Word. I had always believed in Jesus but had never given my life totally to Him — His way. I had never understood the biblical concept of redemption. My relationship with God had been lived under the law of Moses. In Romans and Galatians, I read that no one who lived under the Old Testament laws (the Ten Commandments and an earthly priesthood) could be justified (just as if they had not sinned) by this law before God:

> Therefore by the deeds of the law no flesh will be justified in His sight, for by the law is the knowledge of sin (Romans 3:20).

> But that no one is justified by the law in the sight of God is evident, for "the just shall live by faith" (Galatians 3:11).

Under the law of the Old Covenant, the offering of animal sacrifices could not take away sins, "For it is not possible that the blood of bulls and goats could take away sins" (Hebrews 10:4). Under the old covenant, priestly offerings could not take away sin; therefore God remembered the peoples' sins again and again:

> And every priest stands ministering daily and offering repeatedly the same sacrifices, which can never take away sins. But this Man [Jesus], after He had offered one sacrifice for sins forever, sat down at the right hand of God (Hebrews 10:11-12).

According to the above scriptures, sins were forgiven as long as the sacrifices were offered that God required. Those who lived under the old covenant were in a foreign state for a period of time. Under the law, there was nothing a sinner could do to rid himself permanently from the guilt of his wrongs.

I was saddened when I read in Hebrews that no sacrifice could satisfy God other than the offering of Christ on a cross at Calvary. In Romans 5:8-9 Paul wrote these heart-felt words:

> But God demonstrates His own love toward us, in that while we were still sinners, Christ died for us. Much more then, having now been justified by His blood, we shall be saved from wrath through Him.

The very thought that on the cross of Calvary Jesus paid the penalty for all my sins and provided the way for me to stand before a righteous and holy God fills me with inexpressible gratitude! His sacrifice for me and all of this sin-filled world, stirs me with a deep sense of love and loyalty.

The biblical accounts of the crucifixion of Jesus are told simply in few words. According to Matthew 27:26 and Mark 15:15, Jesus was scourged — stripped and beaten mercilessly. Using a leather whip studded with bits of metal, the soldier administering the beating could literally tear the flesh off a person's back. I doubt if I could have undergone such horrible and excruciating pain. Mental torture was also heaped on Jesus' physical anguish in order to compound His agony. John tells how the soldiers in charge of Jesus' execution began to mock Him, placing a crown of thorns on His brow and draping a purple robe over His bleeding shoulders. They taunted Jesus saying: "Hail, King of the Jews!" As if this wasn't enough, they slapped His face and spat on Him (John 19:1-3).

Death by crucifixion was the worst kind of punishment anyone could receive under Roman law. John tells us in 19:4-16 that after a final attempt at appeasing an angry crowd, Pontius Pilate consented to Jesus' death at a place called Golgotha. Jesus was stripped of His clothing and His hands or wrists and feet or ankles were nailed to this wooden cross.

In the midst of His pain and humiliation, Jesus thought of others rather than Himself. No fighting, screaming, or cursing came from the depths of His pain. He prayed for His executioners saying, "Father, forgive them, for they do not know what they do" (Luke 23:34). Knowing the despondency His mother must have been experiencing by all that was happening to her son, He asked one of His disciples to care for her after His death (John 19:27). Finally, at about 3 o'clock in the afternoon, He cried with a loud voice saying, "Father, into Your hands I commit my spirit" (Luke 23:46). Jesus then took His last agonizing breath and died. Mark records Jesus' crucifixion occurred at 9 o'clock in the morning and His death at 3 o'clock in the afternoon after six torturous hours hanging on the cross.

Christ died the most horrible death imaginable in order to turn God's wrath from me. He became the price paid for my redemption. Before Christ came, my condition was one of alienation and separation from God. As Isaiah said, "But your iniquities have separated you from your God" (Isaiah 59:2).

Whenever I recall Jesus' death, my conscience sharply feels the stain, defilement, and shame of sin. I am plagued with regret and remorse. Like the crowd who had crucified Jesus and later became aware of their sin (Acts 2:36-38), I cry out, "What must I do to be saved?" The answer comes back, "Humble yourself. Trust in me and my word and stop relying on the merits of your good works and the power of all your rituals. Come and wash away all your sins in the watery grave of baptism, and I will bury those sins in the deepest part of the ocean to remember them no more. Your soul will become as white as snow. I sent my only Son to suffer and die for you so that you can become reconciled with me. I love you that much!"

> For I will be merciful to their unrighteousness, and their sins and their lawless deeds I will remember no more (Hebrews 8:12).

> But if we walk in the light as He is in the light, we have fellowship with one another, and the blood of Jesus Christ His Son cleanses us from all sin (1 John 1:7).

I could not reject such a gracious and loving offer, knowing that I would receive the gift of everlasting life!

> Or do you not know that as many of us as were baptized into Christ Jesus were baptized into His death? Therefore we were buried with Him through baptism into death, that just as Christ was raised from the dead by the glory of the Father, even so we also should walk in newness of life (Romans 6:3-4).

My deep faith in God started the conversion process; the Word of God was implanted in my mind and heart and began to change my thinking and a desire for reconciliation before God. Finally, baptism changed my relationship with God and allowed me the right of eternal happiness with God.

The Catholic Church teaches that Jesus died for my sins, yet it substitutes the Mass to show the substitutionary death of Jesus for one's sins. Through the study of God's Word, I now understand that this concept disregards the biblical teaching that Jesus sacrificed Himself once and for all time as full payment for all my sins at Calvary. As a

Catholic, I had been taught that Jesus did not die as a penalty for sin but rather He died to give all mankind the opportunity to save themselves. It was therefore necessary that I do my part by maintaining my faith in the traditions of the Catholic Church, keeping the commandments of God and the Church, and leading a good life. Only then, could I merit salvation in heaven. This merit would be achieved through my works, the help of God, and the sanctifying grace I would receive by participating in the sacraments of the church. Unknowingly, I had been living according to many of the laws of the old covenant that had been incorporated into Roman Catholic theology.

God fulfilled the first term of the new covenant with me by putting His laws into my mind and heart. According to the second term of the covenant, "and I will be to them a God," I had to meet His requirements for this to occur. Paul says in Galatians 4:28, "Now we, brethren, as Isaac was, are children of promise."

Because of Christ's offering, I am in a right relationship with God and am now of the truth faith. In John 1:13 I'm told that I am now "born, not of blood, nor of the will of the flesh, nor of the will of man, but of God."

Another promise of the new covenant God made with me was that the blood of Christ would cleanse me thoroughly from all my sins each time I approached the throne of grace:

> If we confess our sins, He is faithful and just to forgive us our sins and to cleanse us from all unrighteousness" (1 John 1:9).

The grace (or gift) of God brought me out of a watery grave and restored me to life so that all I had lost because of sin has now been regained in Christ. I no longer have to merit my salvation, for God tells me in Ephesians 2:8-9:

> For by grace you have been saved through faith, and that not of yourselves; it is the gift of God, not of works, lest anyone should boast.

God's wonderful grace is His unlimited and undeserved love expressed in active good will toward sinners like me.

Today I rejoice as one of His royal priests, (2 Peter 2:5, 9) appointed by God to offer Him gifts and sacrifices (Hebrews 5:1; 8:3). I cannot come before God's presence with the bodies of beasts as the priests did under the old covenant, but I can come presenting my own body as a living sacrifice before His throne, made pure through the blood of Jesus:

> I beseech you therefore, brethren, by the mercies of God, that you present your bodies a living sacrifice, holy, acceptable to God, which is your reasonable service (Romans 12:1).

In reverential love and gratitude, I must give of myself daily as a spiritual worship:

> Therefore by Him let us continually offer the sacrifice of praise to God, that is, the fruit of our lips, giving thanks to His name. But do not forget to do good and to share, for with such sacrifices God is well pleased (Hebrews 13:15-16).

As a member of God's royal priesthood I must also suffer for and serve others, as did my Savior who "did not come to be served, but to serve" (Matthew 20:28). Peter captures this concept when he says:

> For to this you were called, because Christ also suffered for us, leaving us an example, that you should follow His steps (1 Peter 2:21).

As a priest of God, I am, of necessity, a minister (servant) of Jesus Christ. The biblical concept is that every Christian is a priest and a minister (servant) of Jesus Christ. The word translated minister is derived from the word *diakonos* which occurs 30 times in the New Testament and is rendered minister 20 times, deacon three times, and servant seven times. The word simply means a "servant."

Every Christian is a part of God's clergy. In ecclesiastical usage the word "clergy" is used to designate a small but powerful minority in a religious body. The word "clergy" comes from the Greek word *kleroo* which means "a lot or an inheritance." In Ephesians 1:11 the word is used as "inheritance":

> In Him also we have obtained an inheritance, being predestined according to the purpose of Him who works all things according to the counsel of His will.

This word refers to the entire church. It is evident that the biblical usage of the *kleroo* contrasts sharply with the current use of the English word "clergy." All baptized believers are included within His "heritage" or "clergy."

The word "laity" comes from the Greek word *laos* which is translated "people" in the Bible. This word is used 141 times in the New Testament, and it simply refers to the entire body of obedient believers. For example, this word appears in 1 Peter 2:9:

> But you are a chosen generation, a royal priesthood, a holy nation, His own special people [*laity*], that you may proclaim the praises of Him who called you out of darkness into His marvelous light.

Each priest is a living stone, precious and significant in God's sight (1 Peter 2:4-5). As one of God's living stones our value is enhanced by joining with others to form a house. This house functions best when its parts are fitted together for each other's needs and protections (Ephesians 2:19-22).

The church is a creation of God, and He is the center of its life. This is evident in Peter's description of the church's worth (1 Peter 2:9). This passage makes four points:

1. The church is a chosen race — God's choice of a people for His redemptive witness.

2. The church is a royal priesthood — a kingdom in which every subject is a priest.

3. The church is a holy nation — a people set apart to bear the name and nature of the holy God whom they worship and serve.

4. The church is God's own people — His cherished possession.

Priestly functions arise out of the church's relationship to Christ. Committed to proclaiming a ministry of reconciliation (2 Corinthians 5:18-19), the church is a fellowship rising above the things that fragment humanity.

God's people are not to be passively occupying the perimeter of Christ's kingdom. This divinely called laity is God's royal priesthood! The privilege of declaring His excellencies is ours to enjoy. With our lips and our lives we are to show forth His wonderful deeds and herald the good news of the gospel.

Some 57 generations ago, Paul wrote in Romans 1:16: "For I am not ashamed of the gospel of Christ, for it is the power of God to salvation." Just as my spiritual brother Paul was bold in sharing the truth he had learned from his conversion to God's Word, each of us must also declare the good news of Jesus to a hopeless and dying world.

I am burdened by the confusion and apathy of those bound by religious traditions and man-made rules. I am acutely sensitive to their hurts, pain, ignorance of God's will, and commitment to cultural traditions and unscriptural teachings. As one of God's priests, I want them to know that He will not accept any of the following excuses on Judgment Day:

I am too busy. I am afraid to make a decision. It isn't a convenient time. There are too many hypocrites in the church. I am not sure I need to. I don't believe God will condemn me, He's too loving a God to damn anyone. I'm doing the best I can. I have my own opinions about being saved. How do I know there's a God. I have plenty of time. Some church people once did me wrong. My parents object to me going. All they do is ask for money. The Bible is too difficult to understand. I'm not sure which church is the right one. No one can be sure of salvation. Only the priest or preacher can interpret the scriptures.

All of these excuses fall short of being justifiable reasons for not obeying God's Word. The one thing that will matter will be that each of us listened, repented, obeyed, and faithfully followed until that final day.

The message that should affect my life and yours today is the message of the cross. The forgiveness of sin was not without great cost to God and to His Son, Jesus Christ. The horrors of the indignities Jesus suffered in unjust trials, the brutalities He incurred at the hands of calloused bullies, and the agonies He withstood through six hours of excruciating pain nailed to a cruel wooden cross were the price He paid for our sins. The death of Jesus to save us from our sins is largely beyond our understanding, but it is not beyond our caring and our response in faith and love and obedience to Him.

Had you been one of the crowd that stood near Jesus and heard His dying words, would you have grasped their full meaning? Would you have understood what Jesus meant when He said, "But seek first the kingdom of God and His righteousness, and all these things shall be added to you"? Would you have fallen on your knees in complete surrender to Jesus? When you and I stop trusting in ourselves, our good works, and our own moral goodness and allow Jesus to become the Lord of our lives, our surrender will be complete.

We live in troubled times — days of uncertainty, religious division, confusing philosophies, doctrinal error, and natural disasters of every kind. Jesus came to this earth, so that you and I might have life and have it more abundantly. He died to save us from a wasted life. Jesus wants to fill the emptiness and loneliness that exist in our lives. He wants each of us to come to Him in simple faith and obedience. He promises that our burdens will be lifted and our voids filled when He says:

> Most assuredly, I say to you, he who hears My word and believes in Him who sent Me has everlasting life, and shall not come into judgment, but has passed from death into life (John 5:24).

One day each of us will give an account of our response to God's Word. Jesus spoke of this day when He said:

> He who rejects Me, and does not receive My words, has that which judges him — the word that I have spoken will judge him in the last day (John 12:48).

Paul spoke frequently of the coming judgment day:

> Truly, these times of ignorance God overlooked, but now commands all men everywhere to repent, because He has appointed a day on which He will judge the world in righteousness by the Man whom He has ordained. He has given assurance of this to all by raising Him from the dead (Acts 17:30-31).

> For we must all appear before the judgment seat of Christ, that each one may receive the things done in the body, according to what he has done, whether good or bad (2 Corinthians 5:10).

Jesus gives us a further glimpse of the conversation that will take place on that great day:

> Many will say to Me in that day, "Lord, Lord, have we not prophesied in Your name, cast out demons in Your name, and done many wonders in Your name?" And then I will declare to them, "I never knew you; depart from Me, you who practice lawlessness" (Matthew 7:22-23).

It is very difficult for many of us to believe that religious people or miracle workers will be lost in the hereafter. We ask, "Why?" Jesus gave us the answer when He proclaimed:

> Not everyone who says to Me, "Lord, Lord," shall enter the kingdom of heaven, but he who does the will of My Father in heaven (Matthew 7:21).

Thus we see that it is not enough to call Jesus Lord. It is not enough to do wonderful works in Jesus' name. We will be lost forever if we fail to do God's will. When the will of the Lord is changed by men, it ceases to be the will of the Lord and becomes the will of men. Anyone who changes, adds to, or takes away from the will of God will be cast from God's presence on that great judgment day.

The Bible teaches that our words and deeds will be judged by the words of Jesus. What will you say at the judgement? If you are a member of God's royal priesthood you can be assured of eternal life, for:

> There is therefore now no condemnation to those who are in Christ Jesus, who do not walk according to the flesh, but according to the Spirit. For the law of the Spirit of life in Christ Jesus has made me free from the law of sin and death. For what the law could not do in that it was weak through the flesh, God did by sending His own Son in the likeness of sinful flesh, on account of sin: He condemned sin in the flesh, that the righteous requirement of the law might be fulfilled in us who do not walk according to the flesh but according to the Spirit (Romans 8:1-4).

Epilogue
Salvation — God's Success Formula for a Royal Priesthood

〜〜〜

We all need the eternal hope that Christ provides "as an anchor of the soul, both sure and steadfast" (Hebrews 6:19). Only by knowing God and His will for our lives can we be truly and completely happy. God has a plan for success in your life. If you follow this plan you can be assured that you will become a royal priest and receive the following blessings:

1. The assurance of the pardon of your sins (Acts 2:38).

2. The assurance that God will hear your prayers (1 Peter 3:12).

3. The assurance that God will not allow you to be tempted beyond your ability to bear your struggles (1 Corinthians 10:13).

4. The assurance that Jesus, who "was in all points tempted as we are" (Hebrews 4:15), understands all your problems and is touched with the feeling of your infirmities.

5. The assurance that Jesus shares your cares and burdens (1 Peter 5:7).

6. The assurance that "all things work together for good to those who love God, to those who are the called according to His purpose" (Romans 8:28).

7. The assurance that the Holy Spirit helps in your weaknesses (Romans 8:26).

8. The strength and comfort of association and worship with fellow Christians (Hebrews 10:24-25).

9. The privilege of belonging to a royal priesthood (1 Peter 2:9).

10. The assurance of life everlasting (Revelation 14:13; 21:4).

The following requirements are needed for this formula to become operative in your life:

Recognize Your Sinfulness

Agree with God that you are a sinner unable to save yourself: "But your iniquities have separated you from your God; And your sins have hidden His face from you, So that He will not hear" (Isaiah 59:2).

Believe on the Lord Jesus Christ

The Bible tells us that once you recognize that God is holy and no sin will ever enter His presence for "righteousness and judgment are the foundation of his throne" (Psalm 97:2), God requires that you believe in His Son, Jesus:

These things I have written to you who believe in the name of the Son of God, that you may know that you have eternal life, and that you may continue to believe in the name of the Son of God (1 John 5:13).

But as many as received Him, to them He gave the right to become children of God, to those who believe in His name (John 1:12).

And truly Jesus did many other signs in the presence of His disciples, which are not written in this book;

but these are written that you may believe that Jesus is the Christ, the Son of God, and that believing you may have life in His name (John 20:30-31).

Profess Your Faith

Faith in Jesus is the key factor:

But without faith it is impossible to please Him, for he who comes to God must believe that He is, and that He is a rewarder of those who diligently seek Him (Hebrews 11:6).

This faith does not come by some mysterious feeling or experience, but rather "faith comes by hearing, and hearing by the word of God" (Romans 10:17). You must stop believing in your good works or your moral goodness and trust in Jesus alone for your eternal salvation.

Repent of Your Sins

Repentance is a change of mind that leads to a change of conduct. Without repentance, no one can know God.

I tell you, no; but unless you repent you will all likewise perish (Luke 13:3).

[A]nd that repentance and remission of sins should be preached in His name to all nations, beginning at Jerusalem (Luke 24:47).

Truly, these times of ignorance God overlooked, but now commands all men everywhere to repent (Acts 17:30).

Then Peter said to them, "Repent, and let every one of you be baptized in the name of Jesus Christ for the remission of sins; and you shall receive the gift of the Holy Spirit" (Acts 2:38).

Confess Your Faith in Christ

You must publicly state your submission to the Lordship of Jesus:

He said to them, "But who do you say that I am?" And Simon Peter answered and said, "You are the Christ, the Son of the living God" (Matthew 16:15-16).

Therefore whoever confesses Me before men, him I will also confess before My Father who is in heaven (Matthew 10:32).

[T]hat if you confess with your mouth the Lord Jesus and believe in your heart that God has raised Him from the dead, you will be saved. For with the heart one believes unto righteousness, and with the mouth confession is made unto salvation (Romans 10:9-10).

Then Philip opened his mouth, and beginning at this Scripture, preached Jesus to him. Now as they went down the road, they came to some water. And the eunuch said, "See, here is water. What hinders me from being baptized?" Then Philip said, "If you believe with all your heart, you may." And he answered and said, "I believe that Jesus Christ is the Son of God" (Acts 8:35-37).

Be Buried in the Waters of Baptism

Baptism completes the initial response of faith. Jesus instructed His disciples to teach people and to baptize them (Matthew 28:18-20). Peter emphasized the importance of baptism in salvation:

There is also an antitype which now saves us — baptism (not the removal of the filth of the flesh, but the answer of a good conscience toward God), through the resurrection of Jesus Christ (1 Peter 3:21).

Baptism — immersion in water — is a likeness of the death, burial, and resurrection of Christ (Romans 6:5). Baptism marks your death to sin and your resurrection to walk in a new life. In this moment of submission you are united with Christ and reconciled with God. Jesus said:

Most assuredly, I say to you, he who hears My word and believes in Him who sent Me has everlasting life, and shall not come into judgment, but has passed from death into life (John 5:24).

I encourage you to commit yourself to God, study His Word, do what He says, and claim your place as one of His royal priests.

A Summary of Roman Catholic Practices
And the Approximate Dates of Their Institution[20]

Baptism as a saving ordinance A.D.	150
Infant baptism	225
Lord's Supper as an elaborate sacramental sacrifice	250
Prayer's for the dead	300
Making the sign of the cross	300
Worship in Latin language	600
Temporal, political power of the Pope	754
Worship of Mary and Saints	788
Worship of the cross, images, and relics	788
False Decretals of Isidore	847
Donation of Constantine	858
Baptism of bells	965
Fasting on Fridays and in Lent	998
Fabrication of holy water	1000
Rosary Beads	1090
Money for masses	1100
Enforced celibacy of priests	1123
The Inquisition	1184
Sale of indulgences	1190
Transubstantiation of the wafer	1215
Auricular confesstion of sins to the priest	1215
Adoration of the wafer	1220
The Roman Church as the only Catholic Church	1303
Cup denied to laymen (Council of Constance)	1415
Purgatory (proclaimed)	1438
Unscriptural decrees of the Council of Trent	1545
Tradition equal in authority to the Bible	1545
Justification by works and not by faith alone	1545
Apocryphal books added to the Bible	1545
Invention of scapulars, medals, edible religious stamps	1600
Immaculate Conception of Mary	1854
Infallibility of the Pope	1870
Papal usurpation of right in mixed marriages	1908
Assumption of Mary	1950

Bibliographic Notes

1. The New American Bible, Preface. Wichita, Kansas: Catholic Bible Publishers, 1970.

2. Can I Really Trust The Bible. Grand Rapids, Michigan: Radio Bible Class Publishers.

3. Loraine Boetlner. Roman Catholicism. Philadelphia: Presbyterian and Reformed Publishing Company, 1962.

4. Matthew F. Kohmescher, S.M. Catholicism Today. New York: Paulist Press, 1980, p. 59.

5. Kohmescher.

6. Lumen Gentium 21-11. De Ecclesia, 22.

7. Gregorian Epistle I, Benediction Edition, 1705, p. 742.

8. Donald Attwater. A Catholic Dictionary. New York: The Macmillan Company, 1958, p. 548.

9. Joseph Zacchello. Secrets of Romanism. Neptune, New Jersey: Loizeaux Brothers, 1948, p. 11.

10. O.C. Lambert. Catholocism Against Itself. Winfield, Alabama: O. C. Lambert, pp. 15-16.

11. Lumen Gentium, 64.

12. Elliot Miller and Kenneth Samples. The Cult of the Virgin. Grand Rapids, Michigan: Baker Book House, 1992, p. 42.

13. Charles Taze Russell. The At-One-Ment Between God and Man. Brooklyn, NY: International Bible Students Association.

14. Ralph Woodrow. <u>Babylon</u> <u>Mystery</u> <u>Religion</u>. Miami: Malkuth Corporation, 1966, pp. 21-26.

15. Loraine Boettner. <u>Roman</u> <u>Catholicism</u>. Philadelphia: Presbyterian and Reformed Publishing Company, 1962.

16. <u>Second</u> <u>Vatican</u> <u>Council</u> <u>Dogmatic</u> <u>Constitution</u> <u>on</u> <u>the</u> <u>Church</u>.

17. Boettner.

18. Alexandra Howe. Letter of August 6, 1989.

19. John Greenleaf Whittier. <u>The Complete Poetical Works of Whittier</u>. Boston: Houghton Mifflin Company.

20. Zacchello, p. 210.

A
Change
of
Habit

THE AUTOBIOGRAPHY OF
A FORMER CATHOLIC NUN

Old habits are hard to change — especially those that define your relationship with God. In her first book, *A Change of Habit*, Joanne Howe weaves a tapestry of zeal, rigorous discipline and the shattered beliefs of a mature woman who left her vows as a nun to search for spiritual fulfillment. Joanne's narrative brims with emotion and the richness of her experience will linger long after the book is closed. Join the thousands who have been inspired by this true story of a woman who searched for and found a relationship with God.